Contents

Companion website and audio 4

The author 4

Acknowledgements 4

Copyright 4

Introduction and About the Exam 5

Top ten tips 6

Unit 4 – An Overview 10

Content 10

Taking the exam 10

Unit 4 – Section A: Listening 12

Exercises 12

Unit 4 – Section A: Specimen Questions 18

Unit 4 – Section B: Historical Study – Area of Study 1 (set work) 27

Revising Elgar – making revision notes 27

Writing essays – accessing the marks 43

Revising Shostakovich – making revision notes 45

Writing essays – accessing the marks 59

Unit 4 – Section C: Historical Study – Area of Study 3 (selected topic) 62

Writing essays – accessing the marks 62

Area of Study 3a: English Choral Music in the 20th century 63

Area of Study 3b: Chamber Music from Mendelssohn to Debussy 65

Area of Study 3c: Four Decades of Jazz and Blues 1910 to 1950 67

Unit 5 – Developing Musical Ideas 69

Brief A – question 1 70

Brief A – question 2 70

Brief B 71

Brief C 72

Unit 6 – A Musical Performance 73

Solo acoustic performance 73

Technology I: Sequencing 74

Technology 2: Multi-track or close microphone recording 74

Answers for Unit 4 – Section A: Listening 75

Answers and comments on exercises 75

Answers for specimen questions 85

Glossary 88

Companion website and audio

Digital audio accompanies the various exercises throughout this book. Access the tracks by going to our website at www.rhinegoldeducation.co.uk/myrhinegold. Once you have registered, enter the following code to unlock the supplementary resources for this book: 1FACPV

In addition, we have created a YouTube playlist for easy access to the music used for the specimen questions. Search YouTube for Rhinegold Education to find our channel, or scan the QR code below to go straight there. Shortened URLs have also been provided in the book.

The author

Richard Knight read music at St John's College, Oxford, and has been Director of Music at two leading independent schools. He now combines teaching with a position as a senior examiner with one of the A level boards and is also on the examiner panel for the ABRSM. He has written several books for Rhinegold Education including study guides for GCSE, AS and A2. Richard is also a composer with a diverse range of works to his name, including opera, oratorio and chamber music.

Acknowledgements

The author would like to thank the Rhinegold editorial and design team for their expert support in the preparation of this book.

Copyright

Introduction and About the Exam

You will already have gained your AS qualification in music with AQA. To convert this into a full A level, you will need to complete the following units:

- Unit 4: Music in Context (worth 40% of A2 marks)
- Unit 5: Composing: Developing Musical Ideas (worth 30% of A2 marks)
- Unit 6: Performing: A Musical Performance (worth 30% of A2 marks).

Your marks for these units will then be combined with your AS result in an equal weighting to give a final A level result. Therefore, if you were disappointed with your AS grade and are hoping for a higher final mark this year, you need to make a special effort to improve sufficiently for your average to go up by the desired margin.

Take special note that the marks at A2 are apportioned differently from those at AS. At AS, 40% of the marks were for performing, whereas for A2 40% are for the written paper (Unit 4). This extra 10% on the written paper is for Sections B and C, so your knowledge of your set work and chosen special topic need to be strong, and your essay-writing skills more advanced.

The focus of this revision guide will primarily be on Unit 4. In particular you will find:

- Material to help you prepare for the listening questions in Section A
- Analytical information on the set works in a special revision format for Section B
- Revision notes on music relevant to each of the various options in Section C
- Advice on how to write good essays for questions that you will answer in Sections B and C.

Also in this book you will find advice on making final preparations for submitting your work for Unit 5, and some help for approaching the Unit 6 performance.

Remember: your final result does not only reflect how musical, intelligent and enthusiastic you are. A large factor in your mark is how well you have done what the AQA specification requires. There are no marks available for the fantastic performance you gave in the leavers' concert at your school, how many books you have read about your prescribed works, how many hours of listening to music you have put in over the past six months, or the hours you have spent preparing for a big gig with your band. The examiners can only give marks for how well you have done the tasks required of you in the AQA specification, and they can only do this according to their published mark schemes.

This book is intended to help you access as many of those marks as your other skills allow and not trip up over the process of taking the exam.

For some of you, this will be the last step in your music education. For others it will be the stepping-stone to three or four years of studying music at university or music college. Either way, you will want to be as well prepared as possible to make the most of the opportunity.

Good luck!

Top ten tips

You will have trodden a very similar path to this one last year and should have already got into good habits for the AS examination. The following tips will remind you how to go about your exam preparation. They can also help you to get better prepared this year than you were last year. If you were disappointed with your AS result, you should consider carefully how to use them to improve this time around.

1. PLAN YOUR USE OF TIME

Units 5 and 6 have the same deadline for submitting your work: 15 May. You will also have Unit 4 study coming to a climax about this time (and you may soon be on study leave and have no further lessons with your teacher). In addition, you will have your other subjects to think about at this very intense time. You do not want to leave too much to do at the last minute.

Perhaps as early as Christmas, you should consider the amount of time available to you for preparing for all the various aspects of the A2 specification and organise some realistic targets that will create a balanced approach. In particular:

- When are you going to complete the performing unit, and how are you going to schedule your practice beforehand?
- When are you going to complete the composing unit, and when will you write your Review?
- When might you tackle some practice timed essays for Unit 4, and when will you revise for these?

2. REGULARLY TRAIN YOUR EAR

40% of the marks on the Unit 4 paper are available in Section A: the listening questions. How did you fare in the AS listening? Are you hoping to do better this year? It is very unlikely you will do well if you leave preparing for this to the last minute because the relevant parts of your body (your ears and brain) need training. You may have found that the AS questions last year expected knowledge with which you were unconfident; for instance, identifying instruments by their sound, spotting modulations or hearing specific melodic intervals or cadential patterns. You cannot gain confidence in all of these areas from a couple of evenings of intense revision. Instead, your confidence will develop over time if you are regularly listening to, and thinking about, music over a long period of time before you sit this exam. Remember: listening is not the same as hearing. Having music on in the background while you are thinking about something else is hearing; listening means you are concentrating solely on the sounds reaching your ears.

3. LISTEN TO A WIDE RANGE OF MUSIC

The examiners have a huge range of music that they can draw on for Section A questions. In the 2010–12 papers there were questions based on music by Boyce, Purcell, Haydn, Mozart, Berlioz, Chopin, Reicha, Sullivan, Tchaikovsky, Sibelius, Prokoviev and Bartók, as well as more 'easy listening' tunes such as 'A Nightingale Sang in Berkeley Square' and Rodney Bennett's film score for *Murder on the Orient Express*. The more you listen to (not simply hear) and think about music from across a similarly wide range of styles, the less chance there is that you could be caught out in the exam by something unfamiliar to you.

These days, there is a universe of musical performance freely available on YouTube, where you can hear the music and see it being played at the same time so your eyes can reinforce what your brain is listening to. Another good resource is the Naxos listening library at www.naxosmusiclibrary.com – see if your school subscribes to this.

4. LISTEN REGULARLY TO YOUR SET WORK

You will be doing lots of analytical study of your set work, which is important. However, ultimately music is an aural experience and you should be making yourself fully familiar with the musical experience of listening to the symphony you are studying (Elgar Symphony No. 1 or Shostakovich Symphony No. 5). Listening to it regularly should cement in place your understanding of the analytical detail you have studied as you will associate the theory with the sound and musical effect.

Best of all, make sure you attend a professional performance of your set work. Both pieces are repertory pieces of all main orchestras, so there may well be a performance you can get to during your A2 year.

5. USE YOUR INSTRUMENTAL SKILLS TO PLAY YOUR SET WORK

Whatever instrument you play, you can engage with your set symphony practically. It is unlikely that you will play in an orchestra that will be working on such technically challenging works (unless you are in the NYO) but you can still play or sing parts of them.

If you are studying the Elgar and are an able pianist, you might like to tackle the free piano solo version of it made by Sigfrid Karg-Elert that is available at http://tinyurl.com/http-elgarsymphonyno1-com.

Other instrumentalists, and those studying the Shostakovich, can play (or sing) along to the recording, following the appropriate line in the score. The combination of reading the notation with the concentration required to play the music while hearing the resulting sounds is a tremendous boost to your brain, which has to cope with the challenge of assimilating all the information about your set work.

6. READ YOUR SCORE IN SILENCE, JUST LIKE A BOOK

As you sit reading this revision guide it is not necessary for you to be reading it aloud. The words make sense to your eyes, and – should you wish – you can imagine the sound of someone saying the words out loud as you read. The same should be true for your reading of the musical score of your set work. If you have listened to (not heard) the symphony played often enough, you should be able to read the musical score and imagine inside your head the sound of the orchestra playing the music. This is a huge advantage when you are sitting in the silence of the exam room writing an essay. Let your eyes follow the score at the tempo of the music and enjoy your own personal performance inside your head!

Near to the exam, you may want to follow a 'clean' score, i.e. not the one you have been annotating through your studies. Your teacher may be able to help with this. Alternatively, scores for both symphonies can be found online.

7. CHOOSE A HANDFUL OF SHORT PASSAGES FROM YOUR SET WORK TO KNOW IN DETAIL

Both symphonies are substantial. You have many more pages of score to study this year than last year (when you only had two movements to know) and the musical content is more complicated than in Beethoven's first symphony. It is too big a challenge (and not the best use of time) to attempt to know the analytical detail for every page. You should know how to identify the main themes and structure for each movement, but then choose a handful (six to ten maybe) of passages that last just a few pages (or a minute or so of playing time) to know in detail. Choose these well so that you cover all movements and a range of different emotional contexts. These passages can then be used to answer questions about a range of topics including orchestration, melodic style, harmonic vocabulary, imaginative textures, emotional range or the popular appeal of your chosen symphony.

8. LEARN RELEVANT MUSICAL QUOTES AND USE THEM WISELY

There is absolutely no point spending time writing musical quotes in your Section B essay. The examiners know you have a score in the exam room and will also have their own copies. However, you will need to refer to passages within the score. As neither symphony has bar numbers printed in the score you will have to refer instead to rehearsal figures (e.g. 'four bars after figure 5'). You may also need to be clear which instrumental line is relevant to the point you are making.

In Section C, providing pertinent musical quotes on the manuscript paper provided makes a good impression. It is also a more musical skill than learning bar numbers.

9. MAKE SURE YOUR WRITTEN SUBMISSION FOR UNIT 2 SHOWS YOU HAVE TAKEN CARE

The composing unit does not just depend on how your work sounds: the quality of the written score or annotation also makes a big impression on the examiner. In addition, unlike at Unit 2 in your AS, for Unit 5 there is also the Review, which you need to present well. The mark scheme for this unit is holistic; in other words, you will get a single mark awarded after the examiner has considered these other aspects. You can be sure that the quality of the score/annotation and the Review will play a significant part in that assessment.

If you are doing Brief A, check thoroughly for errors such as parallel 5ths or missing 3rds and make sure that your score for Question 2 is well edited with bowing markings and other performance indications. Some score writing software packages have inbuilt tools that check for parallel 5ths and octaves. If this facility does lead you to make alterations to your solution, make sure you check again after you have made your changes.

If you are doing Brief B or C, make sure that all your musical intentions are clearly visible in your score/annotation, and that the material you are providing allows the examiner to follow the recording with the most helpful score or annotation that you can provide.

The Review should also be well presented and provide insight into decisions that you took regarding structure, key centres, textures and instrumentation.

10. MAKE SURE YOUR RECORDING FOR UNIT 6 IS AS GOOD QUALITY AS POSSIBLE

No matter how vibrant the atmosphere in the room when you perform, or, for those taking the alternative options, how superior your IT resources might be, the examiner will only have the audio recording to assess your work. Make sure that it does you justice.

Unit 4 – An Overview

Content

Unit 4 is tested through a written examination. This lasts for 2 hours and 15 minutes, and comes in **three** sections:

SECTION A: LISTENING

Four questions based on excerpts of unprepared music with short-answer questions, the answers for which are available through careful listening to the music, drawing on your general musical knowledge and experience.

SECTION B: AREA OF STUDY 1

This forms the second half of the Area of Study you did for AS, and is similarly based on a set work.

You will be studying one of two set works: either Elgar's Symphony No. 1 or Shostakovich's Symphony No. 5. There will be **two** essay questions on each of these two symphonies. You should ignore the questions on whichever symphony you have not studied, and choose **one** of the questions on the symphony you have studied.

SECTION C: AREA OF STUDY 3

For each of the three options for this Area of Study there will be **two** essay questions (making six in all). You only have to answer **one**.

Taking the exam

The exam is very similar to the Unit 1 paper that you sat for AS music. It is half an hour longer; the extra time is intended for writing your essays (which, as mentioned earlier, are worth more marks at A2 than at AS). You should aim to get accustomed to writing longer essays.

The exam will start with the listening section. This involves extracts of music being played out loud in the exam room. The invigilators will have a CD and, as the exam starts, one of the invigilators will press 'play'.

The next half-hour (approximately) of the exam is governed by the CD. After the initial announcement on the CD there will be a silence of 3 minutes in which you can read the question paper. In this time:

- You **should** read the questions for Section A carefully. You **may** like to highlight any key words in the questions to help you focus your listening on the important points.

- You **could** look ahead to the essay questions for Sections B and C. You **might** be able to select the title for one of the essays you will be writing later and spend some of this time jotting down some sense of an essay plan.
- **Do not** go into a trance and just wait for the next instruction from the voice on the CD.

The music for each question will be played two, three or four times. This will be stated on the question paper and announced on the CD at the start of each question. Use the gaps between each playing to consider what you need to pay close attention to on the next listening, and to think what possible answers there might be.

When the final playing for the music of question 4 in Section A has finished, there will be approximately 1 hour 45 minutes of the exam left for you to write your two essays (one in Section B, the other in Section C). You therefore need to be prepared to write your best essay answer in about 50 minutes per question.

Make sure you keep an eye on the time, and do not spend too long answering the first essay: there are equal marks available for your Section B essay and your Section C essay.

Should you wish, you may answer Section C first.

Unit 4 – Section A: Listening

The listening section tests both your aural perception and your technical knowledge of musical language. AQA provide a list of terms that you should know and be able to recognise; this can be found on page 20 of the specification.

> **NOTE**
>
> Your teacher may have a hard copy of the specification you can use; alternatively, it is easy to find online at www.aqa.org.uk.

Definitions for these terms can be found in the Glossary on pages 88–94 of this book.

The Glossary includes both the AS and the new A2 terms in order for you to build on what you've already learnt. Before you go any further, you may like to look back to the Rhinegold *AS Music Revision Guide* and the exercises and specimen questions that can be found there (pages 10–24). Of course, after another year of study, there are several additional terms that you are expected to understand and be able to recognise by sound at A2 level. Once you feel confident that you have remembered all the AS listening material, you can work through the following exercises that are designed to cement your understanding of the terms that are new at A2 level. You may also like to look at the glossary on pages 135–136 in Rhinegold's *AQA A2 Music Study Guide* (4th edition) where these terms are introduced.

> **NOTE**
>
> The exercises below are not necessarily A2-style questions, but are designed to improve the focus of your listening and sharpen your understanding of terminology. The specimen questions from page 18 onwards are in more of an A2 style.

Exercises

HARMONY

At AS you were expected to be able to hear the difference between major and minor chords, the distinctive sound of the dominant 7th chord and cadential 6/4 chords. In addition to these, at A2 you are expected to also be able to spot chromatic chords and to hear the difference between three different categories of chromatic harmony:

- Diminished 7th
- Augmented 6th
- Secondary 7th.

🔊 1 EXERCISE 1

Listen to the music in Track 1.

The music is in $\frac{2}{4}$ time. The following chart has one square for each beat. Tick any beat on which you hear a diminished 7th chord:

1^1	1^2	2^1	2^2	3^1	3^2	4^1	4^2	5^1	5^2	6^1	6^2

7^1	7^2	8^1	8^2	9^1	9^2	10^1	10^2	11^1	11^2

🔊 2 EXERCISE 2

Listen to the music in Track 2, then answer the following questions:

a. The music has two beats in a bar. In which bars are there augmented 6th chords?
b. What is the likely time signature for the piece?
c. What rhythmic device is used in bars 10–12?
d. What cadence occurs at the end of the piece?

🔊 3 EXERCISE 3

Listen to the music in Track 3. The melody is as follows:

Now answer the following questions:

a. In which bars (and on which beats) do you hear secondary 7th chords?
b. Which of the secondary 7th chords colours the music with a flat sign?
c. How do bars 3–4 relate to bars 1–2?
d. What cadence occurs in bars 3–4?
e. What cadence occurs in bars 9–10?

◀)) 4 EXERCISE 4

Listen to the music in Track 4. The melody is as follows:

Now answer the following questions:

a. In which bars (and on which beats) do you hear dominant 7th chords in third inversion?

b. Which of these are secondary 7th chords?

c. How do bars 3–4 relate to bars 1–2?

d. Where is a dominant pedal note used for a short time?

◀)) 5 EXERCISE 5

Listen to the music in Track 5. The melody is as follows:

Now answer the following questions:

a. Give bar and beat numbers for two dominant 7th chords in third inversion in bars 1–4.

b. Which of these two chords (in question a) is a secondary 7th?

c. Give bar numbers for two half close cadences (Ic–V).

d. Which of the following is not a secondary 7th chord: bar 5^1, bar 6^1, bar 7^3?

e. In which bar is there an augmented 6th chord?

f. What cadence occurs in bars 15–16? Give the full chord progression for these bars.

g. In which bar is there a diminished 7th chord?

14   UNIT 4 – SECTION A: LISTENING

TONALITY

At A2 you are likely to be asked a question about the tonality of a piece of music through aural discrimination. The most likely answers are major, minor or modal. The specification also suggests that whole tone, bitonal and atonal could feature.

You also have to be adept at spotting modulations. These will most likely start from a major tonic. There are then four possible keys that you might need to spot: the tonic minor, the subdominant, the dominant and the relative minor.

◀)) 6 EXERCISE 6

There are six extracts to listen to. These comprise one for each category of tonality listed above. Listen to the music, and fill in the chart below.

Track	What is the tonality of the music?
6a	
6b	
6c	
6d	
6e	
6f	

◀)) 7 EXERCISE 7

There are four tracks to listen to. These comprise a series of short extracts that modulate from the initial major tonic. Each one starts in G major, and each of the possible options listed previously (the tonic minor, the subdominant, the dominant and the relative minor) is represented. Listen to the music and fill in the chart below.

Track	Music starts in G major. To which key does it modulate?
7a	
7b	
7c	
7d	

HARMONIC DEVICES

◀)) 8 EXERCISE 8

Listen to the music in Track 8, then answer the following questions:

a. What harmonic device is used in the opening four bars for the introduction of the piece?

b. What harmonic device is used for the main section of the piece starting at bar 5?

c. What harmonic device is used for the codetta of four bars that mirrors the introduction?

d. What harmonic device is used in the final bar of the piece?

MELODIC DICTATION PRACTICE

◀)) 9 EXERCISE 9

As in Unit 1 at AS, one of the questions in Section A of Unit 4 is likely to require you to fill in missing notes in a melodic phrase. At A2 this may well involve one or more chromatic notes. If you find this difficult, you are most definitely not alone, but it is a skill you can improve with practice. As an incentive, remember that this is a marks-weighted question: each correct note will earn you a mark.

The following exercise is similar to Exercise 9 in the *AS Music Revision Guide*. You may well want to re-visit that exercise first, but this is not necessary.

The melody opposite is missing its notes for bar 3. There are six different versions of the bar, which you can hear in Tracks 9a–9f. In each case there are **five** notes in the empty bar; the rhythm is always a crotchet plus four quavers.

Remember that chromatic notes add colour to the melody and therefore should stand out when you are listening to them. They will usually resolve by a semitone to a diatonic note: chromatic notes that are sharps are likely to resolve upwards by a semitone; chromatic notes that are flats will probably resolve downwards by a semitone.

Listen to each version **three** times and fill in the missing notes.

(a)

(b)

(c)

(d)

(e)

(f)

Unit 4 – Section A: Specimen Questions

In past papers there have been two slightly different types of question. Most of the questions are similar in style to questions 1 to 3 of the AS Unit 1 paper. This type of question will be familiar to you: an extract of music will be played three or four times over and there are a series of short answer questions.

One of these questions is likely to include some aural dictation: i.e. there will be some missing notes in a melodic line (or, just possibly, the bass line) as printed on a skeleton score, and you have to fill in the pitches of the notes according to the given rhythm. Unlike the AS paper, this may include some chromatic notes (requiring accidentals) so there is an extra dimension to how carefully you need to listen.

The other type of question will play three or four passages from the same work that have a clear similarity (most probably a shared theme). You are asked to describe the differences, using technical vocabulary. The differences may include aspects of instrumentation, tonality, rhythm and metre, tempo and texture. Pieces in variation form are an obvious choice for this type of question; for example, the 2011 paper included a question based on Tchaikovsky's *Rococo Variations* for cello and orchestra.

Here is a set of four standard questions and one comparison question. Answers can be found on pages 85–87.

> **NOTE**
>
> Suggested recordings for YouTube are provided in Rhinegold Education's YouTube playlist, as well as advice on locating the correct passage from other sources. You should play the excerpts the number of times stated in the question, with a gap of 20 seconds between each playing.

Question 1

You will hear an excerpt from William Walton's *Spitfire Prelude*. The music will be played four times with pauses between each playing.

> **NOTE**
>
> Recommended recording:
>
>
>
> http://tinyurl.com/http-waltonspitfire-com
>
> Stop at 1:24.
>
> If you are listening to a recording from a different source, it is the opening of the piece up to the bar before figure 2.

There are two sections to the music:

Introduction   **Main theme**

$\boldsymbol{f/ff}$ $\boldsymbol{mf}$

a. Which family of instruments begins the piece? *(1 mark)*
b. Which is the best description of the bass line for the opening seven bars? *(1 mark)*
- ◼ The bass line rises with a diatonic scale
- ◼ The bass line falls with a diatonic scale
- ◼ The bass line rises with a chromatic scale
- ◼ The bass line falls with a chromatic scale.
c. Which instruments have the countermelody in the second half of the introduction? *(1 mark)*
d. Which two percussion instruments are heard in the introduction? *(2 marks)*
e. On which degree of the scale does the bass finish at the end of the introduction? *(1 mark)*
f. Which of the following is the opening to the main theme? *(1 mark)*

g. Which new percussion instrument is heard during the main theme? *(1 mark)*
h. Which of the following statements is true? *(1 mark)*
- ◼ The harmony of the main theme is diatonic throughout
- ◼ The harmony of the main theme is diatonic in the first half and chromatic in the second half
- ◼ The harmony of the main theme is chromatic in the first half and diatonic in the second half
- ◼ The harmony of the main theme is chromatic throughout.
i. What cadence is heard at the end of the extract? *(1 mark)*

Total: 10 marks

Question 2

You will hear the opening section of an aria from Purcell's *Ode for St. Celia's Day* (1692) entitled 'Wondrous Machine'. The music will be played three times with pauses between each playing.

NOTE

Recommended recording:

 2

http://tinyurl.com/purcellhail

Start at the beginning and finish at 1:03.

The words are as follows:

> Wondrous machine
> To thee the warbling lute
> Though used to conquest
> Must be forced to yield.

a. Which keyboard instrument is heard in the first 2 bars? *(1 mark)*

b. 2 oboes enter in bar 3. At what interval are they apart? *(1 mark)*

    3rd   4th   6th   octave

c. The solo bass sings the word 'wondrous' four times, to which melodic contour? *(1 mark)*
- A rising major scale
- A rising minor scale
- A rising major arpeggio
- A rising minor arpeggio

d. On which word is the singer's lowest note heard? *(1 mark)*

e. What melodic devise is used on the word 'warbling'? *(1 mark)*

f. Throughout the music there is a ground bass of 16 quavers. Complete the pattern. *(1 mark)*

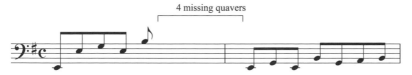

g. What is the tonality of this music? *(1 mark)*

Question 3

You will hear the opening of the second movement of Poulenc's *Concerto Champêtre*. The music will be played four times with pauses between each playing.

> **NOTE**
>
> Recommended recording:
>
> 3
>
> http://tinyurl.com/http-poulencchampetre-com
>
> Stop at 1:15.
>
> If you are listening to a recording from a different source, it is the start of the second movement up to figure 2. Be aware that there are two different versions of this piece that facilitate different solo instruments; the answer to this question might therefore have a different answer.

Here is a skeleton score for the extract:

a. Which best describes the melodic contour in the first bar? *(1 mark)*
- ◼ A rising major arpeggio
- ◼ A falling major arpeggio
- ◼ A rising minor arpeggio
- ◼ A falling minor arpeggio.

b. Complete the melody in bar 7 using the given rhythm. *(5 marks)*

c. What solo instrument enters at bar 17? *(1 mark)*

d. What is the difference between the chord on the downbeat of bar 17 and the one on the downbeat of bar 18? *(1 mark)*

e. Which two instruments enter with the melody at the end of bar 24 (one octave apart)? *(2 marks)*

Question 4

You will hear the opening of Mendelssohn's 'War March of the Priests' from the incidental music he wrote for a play called *Athalie*. The music will be played three times with pauses between each playing.

> **NOTE**
>
> Recommended recording:
>
> 4
>
> http://tinyurl.com/http-mendelssohnwarmarch-com
>
> Stop at 2:33.
>
> If you are listening to a recording from a different source, the excerpt is the start of the march up to bar 68. Other recordings may not use the same repeats; some repeats played in the recommended recording may be omitted, further sections might also be repeated.

The excerpt is structured as follows:

Introduction   Section A   Section B   Section A   Section C

Here is a skeleton score of the excerpt:

Answer the following questions:

a. What instrument begins the piece? *(1 mark)*
b. What chord is used throughout bars 4 to 8? *(2 marks)*
c. What chord is heard on the downbeat of bar 10? *(1 mark)*
d. What chord is heard on the downbeat of bar 15? *(2 marks)*
e. What type of descending scale is used in the melody of bars 21 to 23? *(2 marks)*
f. In what key is Section B? *(1 mark)*
g. What type of cadence occurs in bars 35 to 36? *(1 mark)*
h. What is the key and cadence at the end of the excerpt (section C)? *(2 marks)*

Question 5

You will hear the opening two verses of the fourth song from Elgar's *Sea Pictures* entitled 'Where Corals Lie'. The music will be played three times with pauses between each playing.

NOTE

Recommended recording:

 5

http://tinyurl.com/http-elgarseapictures-com

Start at 13:4 (which is tagged) and finish at 15:4.

If you are listening to a recording from a different source, it is the opening of the fourth song of *Sea Pictures* (in the orchestral version) up to the end of bar 28.

The words are as follows:

> The deeps have music soft and low
> When winds awake the airy spry;
> It lures me, lures me on to go
> And see the land where corals lie;
> The land where corals lie.
>
> By mount and mead, by lawn and rill,
> When night is deep, and moon is high,
> That music seeks and finds me still
> And tells me where the corals lie;
> The land where corals lie.

a. Describe the orchestral texture of the opening phrase of the introduction. *(1 mark)*
b. What is the tonality of the song? *(1 mark)*
c. On which word is a lombardic rhythm (scotch snap) heard in the vocal line? *(1 mark)*
d. A new melodic phrase is heard in the interlude between verses; it is played twice, each time doubled on two instruments, two octaves apart. Give the two pairings. *(4 marks)*

First time: upper instrument _ _ _ _ _ _ _ _ lower instrument _ _ _ _ _ _ _ _

Second time: upper instrument _ _ _ _ _ _ _ _ lower instrument _ _ _ _ _ _ _ _

e. Which two of the following are heard in the melodic line. *(2 marks)*
- ■ A rising minor triad
- ■ A falling major triad
- ■ A falling minor triad
- ■ A rising octave leap
- ■ A falling octave leap.

f. Which solo instrument in the orchestra doubles the voice at the start of verse 2? *(1 mark)*

Question 6

You will hear four extracts from the slow movement of Tchaikovsky's fourth symphony.

> **NOTE**
>
> Recommended recording:
>
> 6
>
> http://tinyurl.com/http-tchaiksymph4-com
>
> The four excerpts from this track that you require are:
>
> - ■ Theme: start up to 0:40
> - ■ First version: 0:40 to 1:21
> - ■ Second version: 2:26 to 3:03
> - ■ Third version: 5:53 to 6:30.
>
> If you are listening to a recording from a different source, the passages are as follows:
>
> - ■ Theme: start up to bar 21
> - ■ First version: bars 21 to 41
> - ■ Second version: bars 77 to 97
> - ■ Third version: bars 199 to 219.

First you will hear the opening melody played by the oboe. This will be played twice. Here is the theme:

a. What harmonic device is used in bars 15 to 21? *(1 mark)*

Three further passages will then be played. You will hear each one three times. Describe how the melody is treated each time, including both the instrumentation of the melody and detail of the texture of the accompaniment.

b. First version *(3 marks)*

c. Second version *(3 marks)*

d. Third version *(3 marks)*

Unit 4 – Section B: Historical Study – Area of Study 1 (set work)

This section of the exam is based on your study of the set work, which will be one of the following two symphonies:

■ Elgar: Symphony No. 1 in A♭
■ Shostakovich: Symphony No. 5 in D minor

The exam tests your analytical understanding of the music and your ability to write well about the piece, choosing examples from the score that suit a given question. You need to be able to describe the construction and effect of the music using a suitable technical vocabulary with confidence. More than was the case at AS, you will also need to understand something of the historical context for the symphony you have studied.

The material here is designed to help you prepare for this section of the exam and, for each symphony, comes in two halves:

■ Firstly, there is advice on structuring your revision notes. This provides you with ready examples for some passages of the symphony and then encourages you to produce similar material for further sections of the symphony of your own choice.
■ Secondly, we look at AQA's mark scheme to gain an examiner's insight into what makes for a good essay style for this exam.

> **NOTE**
>
> Completing your own revision notes will in itself be an excellent way of revising, especially if you follow the examples given below.

Material relating to Elgar's Symphony No. 1 can be found below.

For material relating to Shostakovich's Symphony No. 5, turn to page 45.

Revising Elgar – making revision notes

THE QUESTION PAPER

For your set work study you will have analysed Elgar's Symphony No. 1 in its entirety. In the exam there will be two essay questions from which you must choose **one** to answer. These questions will be numbered 5 and 6 on the exam paper. You will have about 50 minutes to write your answer – quarter of an hour or so longer than the corresponding essay you wrote on your AS set work – which will then be marked out of 30 (rather than 20, as at AS).

Since there are only two questions on the paper for a symphony in four movements, it is likely that there will be two differing approaches:

- One question is likely to give you an opportunity to write in detail on one particular movement, or – perhaps more likely – a set section of one particular movement. For example: *Write an informative account of the exposition in the first movement of the symphony (Figures 5 to 19). You should refer to structure, melody, texture, instrumentation, rhythm, harmony and tonality.*
- The other question is likely to take more of an overview and require you to make your own choice of passages from more than one movement that help to answer the question. For example: Elgar's first symphony is sometimes said to be an example of cyclic form. How important are the thematic links between movements?

Both questions could be challenging to the unprepared candidate. The first clearly requires you to know in detail whichever passage the examiners have set. There will be no marks gained for writing in detail about a section outside figure 5 to 19 however well prepared you are for this. The lesson to be learnt from this is not to skimp on the breadth of what you revise.

The second question requires you to be able to think on your feet: a traditional A level requirement. It is clearly important to write about the way the symphony begins and ends with the motto theme, but how about other links that you have found: the way the scherzo theme transforms into the Adagio theme, or the link between the music at figure 24 during the development of the first movement and the opening of the finale. Again, you will need to have a broad grasp of the symphony as a whole to answer this kind of question.

There is one further catch worth thinking about. For many candidates, the first type of question can seem the more straightforward. Mindful of what happens if the examiners set a passage that is less well known, they revise hard and carefully prepare just about every page of the symphony. On the day, thoroughly well prepared, they can then decide to answer the second type of question to display their comprehensive knowledge. However, if they have never tried to write a music essay of this sort before, they can find it difficult to connect all their knowledge together. It can be difficult to do something for the first time, especially in exam conditions. In this kind of situation, time tends to run away in the exam room, and the result is a poorly structured essay that lacks clarity and a sufficient range of examples. As with all musical skills, this needs practice before you make the critical performance.

YOUR REVISION NOTES

Bearing in mind the two types of question you are likely to find, it is a good idea to compile two sets of revision notes, one for each sort of question. This may sound daunting, but it is well known that learning a fact from two different angles goes a long way to reinforcing the knowledge in one's brain.

You may like to use different coloured paper so that you can be efficiently organised and know exactly where to find your notes for each type of question. It will also help you see what still needs doing when you are midway through your preparation for the exam.

You can also do yourself a big favour by being systematic in how you lay out each page of revision notes. For the first type of question, head up the page with which movement the revision notes refer to, and which section of that movement. Then group information on the page according to the various elements of music: structure, melody, rhythm, harmony and tonality, texture and orchestration. Also summarise the effect of each section of music. Use clear subheadings for each.

Below is an example of how you might apply this advice to the opening passage of the whole symphony.

EXAMPLE REVISION PAGE: FIRST MOVEMENT – INTRODUCTION

Structure: The opening passage is more than just an introduction; it is the 'motto' theme for the whole symphony.

The motto theme is played twice.

Melody: There are two asymmetric phrases – 7 bars + 16 bars – each beginning the same way.

The melody is largely conjunct but with some typically Elgarian leaps such as the rising 6th in its second bar.

The first phrase has the dominant as its topmost note; the second phrase reaches up to the high tonic.

The motto theme is diatonic and ends on the lower tonic.

The motto itself points at a cyclic structure by ending how it started (see three bars after figure 2).

Rhythm: The rhythm of the motto theme is relatively simple: mainly crotchets and three-beat notes. Some of the latter work as ties over barlines to give a yearning, reaching out effect. There are a few dotted crotchet and quaver groupings which give a hint of a formal march character.

The rhythm of the accompaniment is essentially found in the bass line, which is almost totally made of crotchets and suggests a distant march.

Harmony/Tonality: The harmony of the introduction is almost entirely diatonic – there is one use of a secondary 7th – V^7 of V – six bars after figure 3.

Elgar makes frequent use of first inversion triads, a hallmark of his style.

The bass line at the end of the motto theme (both times around) is constructed as a sequential pattern (another of Elgar's hallmarks).

Texture: For the first playing of the motto, the texture is sparse – often just the melodic line and marching bass line with an intermittent third line sometimes present on the horns.

From figure 3 there is a rich homophonic texture, though without the upper register being explored very much.

Orchestration: The first playing of the melody has a distinctive scoring with the melody played in octaves by violas, clarinets, flute and bassoon.

The second time around there is a rich blend of instruments on the tune: first violins and violas, all three flutes, first oboe and all four horns. The bass line is equally full bodied: cellos and basses, bass clarinet and bassoons (including contra) and tuba. The harmony is enriched by the three trombones, with the three trumpets used to highlight each small peak in the music. The timpani are also used with imagination (note dynamics).

Effect: This opening to the symphony is a prolonged period of tonally stable, diatonic music with a long, lyrical melody and a luxuriant orchestral glow that creates an almost nostalgic feel.

There is a sense of it being heard at a distance, or in a restrained way first, and then repeated in more confident colours, before melting away as the introduction ends.

This book is not going to do this process for all the passages you need to learn: you will benefit far more from compiling your own revision notes.

You will recall that the overall structure of the first movement is:

Introduction	First subject	Second subject	Development	First subject	Second subject	Coda
A♭ major	D minor (but unstable)	F major	Various	D minor (but unstable)	A♭ major	A♭ major

In the first movement, passages for which it would be advisable to have revision notes are:

■   The introduction: start to figure 5 – provided above
■   The exposition: figure 5 to19
■   The development: figure 19 to 32
■   The coda: figure 48 to the end of the movement – provided below.

NOTE

The recapitulation for the most part follows the plan of the exposition, and you are less likely to be asked to analyse this. (In any case, if you revise the exposition well, the recapitulation should not catch you out.) Up to figure 35 the main melodic line remains the same, with some differences of orchestration. The main difference is that the second subject, which was heard in F major in the exposition (figure 12), now appears in A♭ major at figure 38. Of course, the first subject in both exposition and recapitulation suggests D minor (in a rather unstable way), but A♭ major was the key at the start of the movement for the motto theme, and that is where Elgar is aiming to finish the movement.

Here is an example of a page of revision notes for the coda.

EXAMPLE REVISION PAGE: FIRST MOVEMENT CODA (FIGURE 48 TO END OF MOVEMENT)

Structure:
The coda is a substantial section – around four minutes long – and provides a counterbalance to the introduction.

There are the following three subsections, almost like a small-scale ternary form:

- Figure 48 to nine bars after figure 51: a tranquil start building to a strong, assured climax at figure 51 and then dying away again
- Nine bars after figure 51 to figure 54: a revisiting or reminiscence of the development with less stability
- Figure 54 to end: tranquillity returns and the movement ends peacefully.

Melody:
At figure 48, we hear the return of the motto theme from the symphony's opening in its entirety, followed (at figure 51) by its opening five notes played twice more. However, the development's opening theme is also present as a countermelody.

From nine bars after figure 51, Elgar returns to the theme with which he began the development – the one that starts with a rising 5th (now in its compound time version). At figure 52 he returns to the angular figure from midway through the development (see figure 24) and four bars later reminds us of the transition idea from figure 10 (in metrically disguised version). Further references back to the development come at figure 53.

From figure 54 Elgar returns to the motto theme; at figure 55 there is also an echo of the closing theme (from figure 17).

Rhythm:
Much of the coda is concerned with the juxtaposition of the simple time ($\frac{3}{2}$) of the motto theme, and the continued presence of the compound time ($\frac{6}{4}$) which first appeared in the transition (figure 9) and which became more to the fore in the development. The latter is still persisting seven bars before the end of the movement.

Harmony/Tonality:
The outer sections of the coda have a sense of tonal stability based in A♭ major, with the inner section being tonally unstable.

However, even as late as figure 55, there is a last touch of uncertainty with three bars that suggest A minor, and the final cadence sees the bass move from D♮ to A♭: the two competing tonal centres of the whole movement, and a fitting way to finish the movement.

Texture:
The return of the motto theme at figure 48 is only one strand of a contrapuntal texture that has other significant strands. These are often doubled at the octave to create a rich orchestral tapestry. The bass line is often significant, especially the entry at figure 50.

After figure 54 the texture becomes increasingly delicate and transparent.

Orchestration: A passage of great ingenuity, including:

- The motto returning on the back desks of each string section at figure 48 (=8 players)
- The harp scale in 10ths at seven bars after figure 48
- The bass line entry reinforced by bass trombone and tuba at figure 50
- *Sul ponticello* tremolo playing (on the bridge) in second violins and violas before figure 53
- The motto theme on a soft blend of flute, clarinet and muted horn at figure 54
- Low staccato bassoons in 3rds five bars after figure 54
- Soft clarinets in 3rds at the end.

Effect: The coda is perfectly judged: the return of the motto theme and the passages of stable A♭ major counterbalances the introduction of the movement; however, the intrusion of reminders of instability, development themes and the unusual final cadence with a **_ppp_** dynamic, makes it clear that only the movement has been finished and that there is still a symphonic argument to resolve.

SECOND MOVEMENT

The second movement comprises three main ideas, for which we can use the shorthand 'scherzo idea' (= first subject), 'march idea' (= second subject) and 'trio idea' (= in lieu of a development). From these, Elgar builds a sonata rondo form:

Exposition

A: Scherzo	F♯ minor	Start to figure 59
B: March	C♯ minor	Figure 59 to 64
A: Scherzo	F♯ minor	Figure 64 to 66

In lieu of development

C: Trio	B♭ major	Figure 66 to 71

Recapitulation

A: Scherzo	F♯ minor	Figure 71 to 73
B: March	F♯ minor	Figure 73 to 75
A: Scherzo	F♯ minor	Figure 75 to 77
Coda	Various	Figure 77 to end

In the second movement, passages for which it would be advisable to have revision notes are:

- The 'scherzo idea': start of movement to figure 59 – provided below
- The 'march idea': figure 59 to 64
- The 'trio idea': figure 66 to 71
- The coda: figure 77 to the end of the movement.

Here is an example of a page of revision notes for the 'scherzo idea' to get you started:

EXAMPLE REVISION PAGE: SECOND MOVEMENT – 'SCHERZO IDEA' (FIRST SUBJECT: START OF MOVEMENT TO FIGURE 59)

Structure:
There is a four-bar introduction before the main theme is presented.

The main first theme is heard twice (repeating at figure 56).

A second section of scherzo-like material starts at bar 57. It is heard twice (repeating at figure 58). This has the role of being the transition in the exposition.

Melody:
The short introduction presents a nervous, twitching motif in the lower strings.

The main scherzo theme comprises seven bars of giddy staccato semiquavers and a two-bar woodwind phrase in quavers. When it repeats the two-bar phrase is played twice.

The transition part of the scherzo is built from a jagged string motif and a pattern of four descending conjunct quavers.

Rhythm:
The unusual 1/2 metre creates a very rapid, flitting quality to the scherzo.

The main seven-bar theme is a virtually continuous flow of staccato semiquavers.

The two-bar phrase is made of quavers but includes some syncopation.

Semiquavers and quavers continue to be set in contrast during the transition, though now heard simultaneously.

Harmony/Tonality: The movement has F♯ minor as its home key: a long way from A♭ major. The harmony is sparse, but there is a sense of a tonic pedal.

Texture:
The texture essentially comprises melodic strands rather than chordal elements. Sometimes these are monophonic and sometimes contrapuntal; for instance, the introductory motif persists under the main scherzo theme.

The repeat of the scherzo theme doubles the melody at the upper octave.

The jagged string motif of the transition is treated to overlapping dialogue between first violins/violas and second violins/cellos.

Orchestration:	Scurrying strings carry the main material.
	Woodwinds (note the use of low flutes) take the subsidiary two-bar phrase.
	The transition is more colourful with use of **_ff_** muted trumpets and a glissando on the harps.
Effect:	The main scherzo idea is played **_pp_**: its rapid staccato character creating a distant whirlwind effect. The music bursts out **_ff_** at the transition: an altogether more fiery and intense passage.

THIRD MOVEMENT

The third movement follows a sonata form design, but with hardly any development section, as is often the case when sonata form is used for a slow movement. The main outline is:

Exposition

■ From the start of the movement to figure 98

Comprising:

■ First subject: from start to figure 94
■ Transition: from figure 94 to 96
■ Second subject: from figure 96 to 98

Development

■ From figure 98 to 100

Recapitulation

■ From figure 100 to 104

Comprising:

■ First subject: from figure 100 to 102
■ Second subject: from figure 102 to 104

Coda

■ From figure 104 to the end of the movement

In the third movement, passages for which it would be advisable to have revision notes are:

■ The exposition: start of the movement to figure 98
■ The coda: figure 104 to the end of the movement – provided below.

On the next page is an example of how the coda revision page might look.

EXAMPLE REVISION PAGE: THIRD MOVEMENT – CODA (FIGURE 104 TO THE END OF THE MOVEMENT)

Structure:
The coda is a single arch-shape passage of music with arch-shaped melodic phrases to match.

Melody:
The coda has its own, unique melody: a phrase that is centred on a rising 7th and finishes with a falling 5th. This is treated sequentially.

Three bars before figure 107, the clarinet refers back to a transition idea (see flute 2 before figure 95).

Rhythm:
The rhythm is not complicated. Interesting features include:

- The pause mark in the fifth bar of the coda on the highest note of the phrase: a kind of written in *rubato* to emphasise the yearning quality of the music
- The elaborate flourish in the clarinet two bars before figure 106.

Harmony/Tonality: The coda is tonally stable in D major (the key of the Adagio) and is largely diatonic in its harmony. A few chromatic inflections creep in with secondary 7th chords; for example:

- The C♮ of a D^7 chord four bars before figure 106 which points to the following G major chord
- The D♯ in the next couple of bars that points to E minor chords.

Texture:
The texture is essentially homophonic, though with a rich string basis derived from *divisi* in all sections and various doublings in octaves and 3rds that this allows. There are some prominent countermelody strands, such as the upper cello line two bars before figure 105.

Orchestration:
Elgar's string writing shows considerable detail, with discreet use of pizzicato, tremolo, mutes and *ponticello*. All this is underlined by some deft touches of scoring in the winds and soft playing on the timpani.

In the last few bars muted trombones supported by low harp distantly insert a figure that looks forward to the finale.

In the final chord, a solitary clarinet seems to hang in the air over the low string chord.

Effect:
A passage of great beauty, radiance and poise.

FOURTH MOVEMENT

The finale is a very skilful adaptation of sonata form that reverses the character of the main sections so that tonal instability characterises the exposition and recapitulation, whereas a passage of tonal stability is found towards the end of the development. All this serves one purpose: to make the coda – when the music finally reaches A♭ major once more, and the motto theme returns – the consummation not just of the movement, but of the entire symphony.

The outline of the movement is:

Introduction (lento)

		From start to 5 bars after figure 111	Begins with reminder of D minor
			Tonally unstable
			A glimpse of A♭ major (figure 110)

Exposition (allegro)

First subject	To figure 113	Suggests D minor
Transition	Figure 113 to 114	Tonally unstable
Second subject	Figure 114 to 116	Suggests B♭ major
Codetta	Figure 116 to 118	Tonally unstable

Development

First section	Figure 118 to 130	Kaleidoscopic tonalities
Second section	Figure 130 to 134	E♭ minor/G♭ major

Recapitulation

First subject	Figure 134 to 136	Suggests E♭ minor
Transition	Figure 136 to 137	Tonally unstable
Second subject	Figure 137 to 139	Suggests G♭ major
Codetta	Figure 139 to 141	Tonally unstable

Coda

Anticipation	Figure 141 to 146	Kaleidoscopic tonalities
Consummation	Figure 146 to end	A♭ major

In the finale, passages for which it would be advisable to have revision notes are:

- The introduction: from the start of the movement to five bars after figure 111 – provided on the next page
- The exposition: from five bars after figure 111 to figure 118
- The second section of the development: figure 130 to 134
- The coda: figure 141 to the end.

What follows is an example of how the introduction revision page might look.

Structure:
This is not just a random slow introduction to a sonata form movement, but structurally significant to the whole symphony:

- It reminds us of D minor – the key that competed for supremacy in the first movement, and shares the same tonic as the third movement.
- It uses themes from the first movement, underlining the cyclic nature of the whole symphony.
- It gives a glimpse of A♭ major and the motto theme: an indication of where the symphony is going to end.

Melody:
The first idea heard in bar 2 is the angular theme from figure 24 in the development of the first movement.

Two important new ideas are presented:

- A theme largely in conjunct staccato crotchets
- An arch-shaped idea first heard on the clarinet after figure 108.

The symphony's motto theme also appears.

Rhythm:
Though the contour is different, the staccato crotchet theme seems to capture the same distant, restless march quality as the bass line at the start of the symphony.

The opening angular shape is treated to rhythmic diminution at figure 110.

Harmony/Tonality:
There is quite a lot of chromatic writing here (both melodic and harmonic). The overall sense is D minor at the start, and also for the first appearance of the staccato crotchet theme. At figure 110 the music then moves to A♭ major for a glimpse of the motto theme, before ending on V♭ of D minor for the allegro to start.

In other words, this is a mirror to the first movement's dual tonal centres.

Texture:
There is a range of textural treatments here, including:

- Imitative entries of the angular shape at the start (bass clarinet – bassoon)
- A homophonic texture for the staccato crotchet theme
- A long melodic strand provided by the motto theme.

Orchestration:
There are plenty of imaginative ideas in the scoring. For instance:

- Strings: use of back desks separately, tremolo, frequent changes of muted/unmuted, high register violins *divisi* in three after figure 110
- Winds: the opening brooding bass clarinet solo, the flourish on flute and bassoon two octaves apart after figure 108 (given an extra glistening quality by the harp glissando), all three flutes in unison in their distinctive lowest register at figure 109, the chromatic scale in 3rds on the clarinets after figure 110

- Brass: the soft chord of horns and tuba in bar 5, the entry of the staccato crotchet idea on **_pp_** trombones before figure 110, use of the horns to support the last desks of strings on the motto before figure 111, the use of the trombones **_p_** to help the blend of the final staccato chord of the introduction
- Percussion: The soft rumbling roll on the bass drum at the start, the use of the timpani to underpin the staccato crotchet idea on the bassoons.

Effect: At the start there is a sense of darkness and mystery. Overall it feels like the calm before the storm, or pre-dawn on some momentous day of hard work and ultimate triumph.

WHOLE SYMPHONY ASPECTS

It is harder to predict what angles the examiners might choose for a second question that looks at the whole symphony as there is no clear limit to how imaginatively they might think. Part of the skill on your part, and something for which the examiners will give credit, is being able to 'think on your feet' and drawing on your knowledge to fit the question. However, you will be best prepared to do this if you have considered at least some of the possible angles. Here is a list of suggestions:

- Examples of Elgar's skilful and imaginative orchestration
- The ways in which Elgar views the symphony as a whole with links between movements
- The extent to which the symphony is 'in A♭ major'
- What makes Elgar's melodic ideas distinctive
- Passages that show the emotional range of the symphony
- Reasons for the symphony's popularity.

When compiling your revision notes for these topics, it is important to avoid writing down everything that might be relevant. Each question could be answered by at least a whole chapter of a book, and you only have 50 minutes to write in the exam. Instead, think of how you will structure the essay and only choose the best examples: ones that you can remember easily.

Here is an example of how a revision page for the first of these topics might look.

EXAMPLE REVISION PAGE: WHOLE SYMPHONY TOPIC – ELGAR'S USE OF THE ORCHESTRA

Strings: The strings are the backbone of Elgar's orchestral writing. The expectation is for a string section of 16.14.12.10.8 and the symphony also requires two harps.

    The violin was Elgar's own instrument, and he writes for the strings with great resource and imagination, making use of the full range of techniques:

- High position on the G-string for passionate tone, e.g. start of the first movement's allegro (after figure 5)

- Use of the high register for sweetness of tone, e.g. the second subject of the first movement (figure 12)
- Off the string staccato (*spiccato*) bowing, e.g. the main scherzo theme of the second movement
- Mutes (*con sordini*), e.g. the end of the third movement
- Tremolo, e.g. the start of the finale
- Pizzicato, e.g. cellos at bar 6 of the finale
- Bowing on the bridge (*sul ponticello*), e.g. in the coda of the first movement (after figure 52).

Each of the subsections of the strings gets opportunity to shine. For example:

- Violas present the motto theme at the start in octaves, supported by some of the winds
- Cellos carry the Adagio melody in their passionate tenor register before figure 101 (third movement)
- Elgar liked the second violins to sit on the opposite side of the conductor to the first violins (where cellos usually sit). This creates a stereo effect that he puts to good use in dialogue passages such as in the finale between figure 127 and 128
- Sometimes Elgar uses the full weight of strings together in unison/octaves: e.g. the *con fuoco* statement of the scherzo theme at figure 64.

Elsewhere he will find some unusual divisions of his string section. For example:

- The use of the eight 'back desk' players (first and second violins, violas and cellos) for the distant appearances of the motto theme, e.g. at the start of the first movement coda (figure 48)
- The use of the entire front arc of strings (including front desk second violins, violas and cellos) to add intensity to the first violins' opening melody in the Adagio.

Elgar writes with considerable flair for his two harps; they often seem to be the 'icing on the cake'. Examples include:

- The two glissandi – one upwards, the other downwards – early in the second movement before figures 58 and 59
- The rippling arpeggios during the luxuriant tonal passage midway through the finale at figure 130
- The pulsating chords at figure 143 that – uniquely – add a triplet crotchet rhythm to the texture here
- The flamboyant downward glissando leading into the final return of the motto theme at figure 146.

Elgar uses the harp in a more subtle way to blend into some delicate timbres, for instance, doubling the descending 6ths in the flutes as the second subject starts in the first movement (figure 12). The triplet quaver pattern accompanying the flutes as the trio section of the second movement starts (figure 66) is another good example.

Woodwinds:

Elgar writes for triple woodwind: three each of flutes, oboes, clarinets and bassoons, with the third player of each team doubling on piccolo, cor anglais, bass clarinet and contrabassoon. This is a standard late Romantic wind section.

Elgar is always concerned with the tonal blend; for example, the motto theme at the start is played by clarinets in octaves (doubling *divisi* violas) with a flute doubling the first clarinet and a bassoon doubling the second clarinet.

In the development of the first movement the woodwinds are more prominent than the strings for a while, presenting arabesque patterns either side of figure 22 in various combinations within the section.

Elgar finds a range of character for each of the individual wind instruments:

- Flutes can sound sweet and dainty (the trio of the second movement, figure 66); can have dazzling fast runs (figure 60 to 61 in the same movement); can contribute a rich, haunting tone in their lower register (figure 109 in the introduction to the finale, for instance) or provide decoration with glittering trills in their upper register (figure 145 as the coda builds towards the final statement of the motto theme).
- The oboes are somewhat less often to the fore, but offer a contrasting colour for a solo phrase at times, for example before figure 38. Elgar also sometimes scores a countermelody in octaves between oboe and bassoon, such as before figure 128 in the finale. One of the most inventive – yet simple – uses of the oboes is in the trio section of the second movement where first oboe and cor anglais sustain **pp** an internal tonic pedal note (B♭) for many bars.
- Clarinets are used with, if anything, even more versatility than the flutes. They are sometimes used to enrich string melody lines in mid register on the violas or cellos, such as with the first movement's first subject (figure 5) or the second subject of the finale (figure 114); sometimes the first clarinet has soloistic moments, such as the start of the development in the Adagio (figure 98). However, Elgar also uses the potential of the clarinet for a sweet, soft timbre, the 3rds at the end of the first movement and the last note of the Adagio being good examples.
- Bassoons are also used in various ways. Of course, sometimes their role is to reinforce the bass line, the recapitulation in the first movement (figure 32) being a good example. Elgar, who taught himself to play the instrument, also uses the distinctive tone of the higher register of the bassoon to give colour to both melodic lines (such as the opening motto theme) and harmonic textures (such as the start of the Adagio). The low register of the bassoon is given

prominence near the end of the first movement with an entry in 3rds for two bassoons under a single clarinet line.

Brass:

Elgar writes for the standard late Romantic brass section of four horns, three trumpets, three trombones and tuba.

- Horns are used in a very wide range of ways. These vary from a single muted horn that provides a discreet harmonic line in the initial presentation of the motto theme after figure 1, to all four horns in unison giving a golden tone to the restatement of the motto at figure 3. When the motto returns at figure 8, it is all the horns alone, this time muted and *pp* for a very distant effect. In the finale at figure 131, the horns provide a four-part harmony that adds richness to the texture despite the *p* dynamic, and then, later in the same passage, make a thrilling *f* final entry of the development before figure 134.

- The trumpets are first used as a highlight instrument in the second statement of the motto theme (figure 3) with detailed dynamics used to make chords swell or fade. Elgar uses mutes on all three trumpets for the appearance of the secondary scherzo theme before figure 58, the combination of mutes, a *ff* marking and *staccatissimo* quavers making for a tight, snappy sound with lots of attack. A little further on (figure 61) all three trumpets, now unmuted, play the climactic entry of the march idea high in their range. Perhaps the most thrilling moment for the trumpets, however, is the eight-bar crescendo on a long held concert C at figure 145 as the music builds inexorably to the consummation of the motto theme to finish the symphony.

- Trombones are used at moments of climax, such as figure 27 where the development of the first movement is at full frenzy. They also provide a rich harmonic texture to the second movement's march idea at figure 73. Along with the tuba, later (after figure 75) trombones and tuba in octaves play the march theme themselves. Elgar also knows, however, that the trombone can make a telling contribution with a very soft dynamic, as at figure 95 in the Adagio; in a movement dominated by rich string tone, the two-bar break for strings before figure 96 is filled with a very still *pp* moment for bassoons, first horn and the three trombones. In the finale, more *pp* sustained chordal writing for trombones is found at figure 132, before – for ten bars – Elgar has the imagination to have them just play on the downbeats, making this noble passage have a sense of slowly throbbing.

- The tuba is often heard in tandem with the trombones, but it is also used in other ways. At figure 131 in the finale, it quietly sustains the bass line along with the contrabassoon under a texture of chords on the horns. At figure 60 it is the sole brass player on an entry of the march idea shared with the bassoons and low strings.

Percussion:	Compared to many early 20th-century orchestral scores, Elgar uses a conservative percussion section of timpani, snare drum, bass drum and cymbals. He also uses these instruments with restraint. Nonetheless, he uses them with precision and to marked effect.

The timpani are used in the opening two bars: a distant rumble just to place the tonic note of the symphony in the air. When the motto is re-stated at figure 3, there is a thrilling p to f roll. Elgar makes use of having pedal timps to retune as the exposition moves away from A♭ major at figure 5. At the end of the development (figure 28) there is a long roll of 17 bars on an F♯ pedal note. The timpani give an incisive edge to the intermittent tonic pedal (also F♯) at the start of the second movement, and similarly contribute to the first appearance of the finale's first new material before figure 108. Right at the end of the symphony (figure 151) they are used with some flamboyance with a three-note alternating pattern in triplet crotchets.

The other percussion instruments are used a lot less, and not at all in the first and third movements. They do, however, bring some colour to moments in the second movement, especially at the height of the march idea at figure 61. The bass drum roll at the start of the finale adds to a mysterious atmosphere, and also intensifies just as the final build up begins at figure 149.

Ten particularly good passages to use for illustrating Elgar's orchestral technique are:

First movement

- The first statement of the motto theme at the start
- The return of the motto theme at the start of the coda (figure 48)
- The end of the first movement (figure 54)

Second movement

- The *con fuoco* statement of the scherzo idea (figure 64)
- The entry of the march idea at figure 73

Third movement

- The opening up to figure 93
- The ending from figure 107

Fourth movement

- The opening up to figure 109
- The final section of the development from figure 130 to 134
- The final statement of the motto theme: figure 146 to 147

Writing essays – accessing the marks

Mark schemes for previous Unit 4 papers are available on the AQA website.

Your essays will be assessed for the following qualities:

- Knowledge and understanding of the music
- Relevance to the question set
- Points supported by reference to the score
- Confident use of specialist vocabulary
- Structure of the argument in your essay
- Writing style.

Bearing these factors in mind, you can see that you want to avoid the following pitfalls:

- Factual inaccuracies and incorrect analytical comment
- Writing about aspects of the music that are not relevant to the question
- Making general points that are not backed up by specific references to the score
- Not using appropriate technical terms, or using technical vocabulary in inaccurate ways
- Starting your essay without a clear sense of the argument you want to make in answer to the question, or spending too long making one point so that you do not have time to make others with equal weight
- Writing with poor spelling or grammar.

Writing good music essays requires practice. In particular:

- The more you have studied the symphony, the more your analytical understanding will be accurate and comprehensive.
- The more angles from which you have considered each movement, the quicker you will locate the best examples that will support the points you make. (Remember: you will not have your own personal copy of the score in the exam room with your annotations in it.)
- The more you use specialist vocabulary in conversation, reading about music, making revision notes and writing about the symphony, the more comfortable and convincing you will be in using technical terms in the exam room.
- The more practice essays you write, the better your writing style will be, and the more confident you will be, helping you to keep to time in the exam.

Therefore, make sure you factor into your revision schedule times when you will practise writing essays.

Above all, it is important to convince the examiners that you can hear the effect of the music you are writing about – as though you have a private performance playing in an earpiece in the exam room. This is much more impressive than just describing what you can see on the page in the score.

TWO PARAGRAPHS TO CONSIDER

Imagine you are an examiner and you are marking two attempts to answer the following question:

Give a detailed account of the third movement of Elgar's first symphony. You should refer to structure, melody, rhythm and tonality.

Candidate A's answer begins like this:

> The third movement (adagio) begins in D major, which is where the second movement ended, so Elgar ties the last note over to become the first note of the Adagio. The opening melody is played by the first violins over chords played by the lower strings and some of the winds such as the bass clarinet in bar 1, the bassoons in bar 2 and the cornets in bar 3. It is a long, flowing theme and there are some complicated rhythms in the theme that give lots of energy to the music. There are a lot of expression marks which make the melody very romantic.

Candidate B's answer begins this way:

> The third movement - the slow movement - is in D major and is structured in sonata form with a minimal development section. It begins with an F# - the tonic of the previous scherzo - tied over, and this becomes the 3rd of the new key: a magical effect. The first subject comprises two long phrases of nine and seven bars respectively. There are many rhythmic intricacies such as syncopation in bars 1, 5 and 6, triplet semiquavers in bar 3 and various tied notes, that give the tune a very tender and flexible quality; there are also various chromatic inflections, such as the E# lower auxiliary in bar 4, which add to the expressive character.

Which of these seem like the candidate is on the way to a high mark? If you thought it was the second you are correct. Here there is a clear addressing of the question (structure, melody, rhythm and tonality), successful use of technical vocabulary, careful referencing to examples in the score by bar number, and comment on the resulting sound of the details mentioned. Better still, have you noticed that the candidate has already created a guide to what else is to come in the essay, by stating simply the structural basis of the movement?

Candidate A has not made a promising start. Have you noticed all the reasons why not? We do not yet know what form the candidate thinks the music is in; there are some factual errors concerning the key of the previous movement and the instrumentation (the writer has mistaken the Italian 'corno' in the score for cornets rather than horns); attention is needlessly being given to instrumentation which is not in the question; rhythm is only referred to in general terms, without technical vocabulary or referencing examples in the score, and the attempt to describe the resulting sound ('lots of energy') strongly suggests that the candidate cannot recall what the music actually sounds like.

There are lots of good warnings here to take heed of in order to ensure you do not fall into the same traps.

SAMPLE ESSAY TITLES

- *Explain the structure of the first movement with references to themes and key centres, highlighting any unusual features.*
- *Write a detailed account of the second movement up to the start of the trio at figure 66. You should refer to structure, texture and instrumentation.*
- *Choose three passages from the finale that have contrasting emotional characters, and explain how Elgar achieves this through use of melody, rhythm, and texture.*
- *How important is the motto theme to the overall structure of this symphony?*

Revising Shostakovich – making revision notes

THE QUESTION PAPER

For your set work study you will have analysed Shostakovich's fifth symphony in its entirety. In the exam there will be two essay questions from which you choose **one** to answer. These questions will be numbered 7 and 8 on the exam paper. You will have about 50 minutes to write your answer – quarter of an hour or so longer than the corresponding essay you wrote on your AS set work – which will then be marked out of 30 (rather than 20, as at AS).

Since there are only two questions on the paper for a symphony in four movements, it is likely that there will be two differing approaches.

- One question is likely to give you an opportunity for writing in detail on one particular movement, or – perhaps more likely – a set section of one particular movement. For example: *Write an informative account of the introduction in the first movement of the symphony (the start up to figure 17). You should refer to structure, melody, texture, instrumentation, rhythm, harmony and tonality.*
- The other question is likely to take more of an overview and require you to make your own choice of passages from more than one movement that help to answer the question. For example: *Shostakovich is widely regarded as the greatest symphonic composer of the 20th century. What aspects of his fifth symphony stand out as being clearly 20th century in style and musical language?*

Both questions could be challenging to the unprepared candidate. The first clearly requires you to know in detail whichever passage the examiners have set. There will be no marks gained for writing in detail about any music after figure 17 for which you are better prepared. The lesson to be learned from this is not to skimp on the breadth of what you revise.

The second question requires you to be able to think on your feet: a traditional A level requirement. You do not have time in 50 minutes to write about every page of the score, so you need to be able to make a speedy selection of a few passages that you can write about from the angle the examiners have set. Also, you need to make sure that you can cover different aspects of music language: where is there a good example of a melody that is clearly of a 20th century character? And harmony? And rhythm, texture and instrumentation? Again, you will need to have a good, broad grasp of the symphony as a whole to answer this kind of question.

There is one further catch worth thinking about. For many candidates, the first type of question can seem the more straightforward. Mindful of what happens if the examiners set a passage that is less well known, they revise hard and carefully prepare just about every page of the symphony. On the day, thoroughly well prepared, they can then decide to answer the second type of question to display their comprehensive knowledge. However, if they have never tried to write a music essay of this sort before, they can find it difficult to connect all their knowledge together. It can be difficult to do something for the first time, especially in exam conditions. In this kind of situation, time tends to run away in the exam room, and the result is a poorly structured essay that lacks clarity and a sufficient range of examples. As with all musical skills, this needs practice before you make the critical performance.

YOUR REVISION NOTES

Bearing in mind the two types of question you are likely to find, it is a good idea to compile two sets of revision notes, one for each sort of question. This may sound daunting, but it is well known that learning a fact from two different angles goes a long way to reinforcing the knowledge in one's brain.

You may like to use different coloured paper, so that you can be efficiently organised and know exactly where to find your notes for each type of question. It will also help you see what still needs doing when you are midway through your preparation for the exam.

You can also do yourself a big favour by being systematic in how you lay out each page of revision notes. For the first type of question, head up the page with which movement the revision notes refer to, and which section of that movement. Then group information on the page according to the various elements of music: structure, melody, rhythm, harmony and tonality, texture and orchestration. Also summarise the effect of each section of music. Use clear subheadings for each.

What follows is an example of how you might apply this advice to the opening passage of the whole symphony.

EXAMPLE REVISION PAGE: FIRST MOVEMENT – EXPOSITION – FIRST SUBJECT AREA (UP TO FIGURE 9)

Structure: Almost from the start there is a sense that the exposition includes development of the material as it is presented. Thus the opening, striking idea of leaps and double dotted rhythms lasts barely more than two bars, but is then transformed, almost like an echo, into the accompaniment pattern for a completely different melody at figure 1.

The violin's figure (dotted quaver + two semiquavers) of bar 3 also soon reappears as part of the main first subject theme four bars after figure 1 and again after figure 3 in a different context.

Another very simple idea that is going to become of huge significance later on is the three repeated 'A's that are discreetly heard at the end of the introductory melody in bar 4.

This approach makes for a very organic symphonic structure. For example, at figure 2 all three of the ideas listed above appear in an adapted fashion within four bars. Similarly, a wandering melodic line played by the first violins four bars after figure 3 (that, innocuous as it may seem at this point, will be used for the climax of the whole movement after figure 36) is heard in the bass line at figure 6 under the introductory jagged melody in the violins.

Melody: The first subject area comprises several very contrasting melodic ideas:

- The very angular idea of the opening two bars
- The falling three-note conjunct motif of bar 3
- The three repeated notes of bar 4
- The main theme at figure 1 that is conjunct and based on a falling Phrygian scale
- The extension to this in bars 8 to 11 that uses all 12 pitches of the chromatic scale
- The long, twisting and wide-compassed melody beginning three bars before figure 4.

Rhythm: There is an equally wide-ranging mix of rhythmic character here, from the severe dotted rhythm of the opening two bars (a 1 and 7/8-beat note followed by a demisemiquaver) to the serene rhythm of the main theme at figure 1 (minim + two crotchets). The most significant rhythms in terms of the movement as a whole, however, are:

- The dotted quaver + two demisemiquavers pattern in bar 3
- The two repeated notes in bar 4 that have the potential to drive onto the third note that is on the strong beat.

Harmony/Tonality: The symphony is described as being 'in D minor'. This is immediately established by the use of B♭ and C♯ in the opening bar. The brief introduction ends on the dominant note, A, and as this resolves onto D there is a clear sense that this is the tonic. This is underlined by the use of a dominant–tonic pattern in the bass for a few bars.

However, it soon becomes apparent that Shostakovich's harmonic palette is going to be far more resourceful and expressive than being confined to the tonic key in a diatonic way. Having established the tonic at figure 1, he darkens it, firstly with the Phrygian inflection in the melody, and then with a lot of 'flat side' harmony.

The chromaticism also allows Shostakovich to explore the use of dissonance to intense emotional affect, especially at the climax around figure 8 where the chord has both F♯ and F♮ in it.

Texture: A range of textures is used in the first subject area.

- The opening bars are in a tight canon, at one-beat distance
- The presentation of the main theme is over a discreetly twitching accompaniment
- The canon returns at figure 2 under an inverted pedal C in the violins

- There is a counterpoint formed between two different melodic ideas at figure 6.

Shostakovich often likes a very open texture with space between lines. Examples include the gap between melody and accompaniment in the strings at figure 1 (no second violins needed) and the bass melody far below the tremolo violins at figure 2.

Orchestration: Shostakovich uses each instrument for its specific tone colour rather than thinking in terms of sections. Thus, though the strings start the symphony, the violas are silent until their subtly different timbre is just right to be included one bar before figure 1. Similarly, the first time the oboe is used (figure 5) it creates an exquisitely poignant moment, supported by clarinets in 3rds (it's their first appearance too) and counterbalanced by a bassoon. First entries of the horns four bars after figure 6 (where the first horn seems to wail) and trumpets after figure 7 are equally telling. The whole effect is quite sparse and intense.

In addition to individual use of instruments, Shostakovich also has an ear for interesting combinations. The use of bassoons in octaves at figure 2 doubled by pizzicato cellos and basses makes for a very dry effect; likewise the high first violins at figure 7 are given considerable extra penetrating clarity by being doubled in unison by flutes and the E♭ clarinet at the top of its range.

Effect: There is a strong sense of tension throughout this first subject produced from the changes between rigorous, forthright music – the strict canon with jagged contour and rhythms at the start, or the intense dissonant climax before figure 8 – and cold, withdrawn music such as the sorrowful, lonely theme at figure 1 or the poignant oboe at figure 5. This juxtaposition creates an unsettling effect.

This book is not going to do this process for all the passages you need to learn: you will benefit far more from compiling your own revision notes.

You will recall that the overall structure of the first movement is:

Exposition

- From start to figure 17

Comprising:

- First subject area: start to figure 9 – starts in D minor
- Second subject area: figure 9 to 17 – starts in E♭ minor

Development

- Figure 17 to 36

Recapitulation

- From figure 36 to end of movement

Comprising:

- First subject (subsidiary material only): figure 36 to 39 – starts in D minor
- Second subject: figure 39 to 44 – starts in D major
- First subject: figure 44 to end of movement (after figure 47) – ends in D minor.

In the first movement, passages for which it would be advisable to have revision notes are:

- Exposition: first subject area (start to figure 9) as provided above
- Exposition: second subject area (figure 9 to 17)
- Development (figure 17 to 36)
- Recapitulation: first subject (figure 36 to 39)
- Recapitulation: first subject to end of movement (figure 44 to end) as provided below.

NOTE

Recapitulation of the second subject largely follows the character of its appearance in the exposition, although it begins in the major key this time.

Here is an example of a page of revision notes for the final section of the movement.

EXAMPLE REVISION PAGE: FIRST MOVEMENT: RECAPITULATION PART 3 – FIGURE 44 TO END OF MOVEMENT

Structure: In a way this passage feels like the coda, but it is also the first appearance of the main first subject theme in the recapitulation and there is little sense of resolution to the symphonic argument at this point.

Melody: The main first subject theme at figure 44 is treated to inversion, but maintains its cold Phrygian colour.

There are a number of fragile-sounding rising scales, initially of a minor colour, and then, in the last three bars, chromatic.

The symphony's initial melodic idea is heard in the bass at figure 46.

Rhythm: The dotted rhythms of the opening are still ominously sounding in the accompaniment, and then just the bass line, before lingering in the low trumpets in the final bars.

Harmony/Tonality: The opening of this section sounds unsettling because the music has not settled on the tonic; instead, for five bars there is a sense of E as keynote.

When the timpani enter to take the music back towards D, the would-be tonic chord on the downbeat is compromised by dissonant notes in the violins (E and B♭). More chromaticism is heard at figure 46. There is no definitive cadence as the movement ends.

Texture: There is a sustained element to this passage with just a few fragile melodic strands. At figure 44 the texture is quite low in register; over this the melodic writing gradually ascends until it is being played on the high, crystal-clear bell sounds of the celesta whilst the dense weight of D minor sounds far below.

Orchestration:	Figure 44: muted strings, low register haunting flute tone.
	Figure 45: delicate solo piccolo – a Shostakovich speciality – then passing to a solo violin high above the accompaniment texture of strings.
	Figure 46: muted horns take over the role of providing the sustaining tone in the texture.
	Figure 47: an ominous deep bass line with timpani and harp, as well as cellos and basses; above this the celesta scales sound like ice crystals.
Effect:	Eerie, mournful, oppressive and strangely beautiful.

SECOND MOVEMENT

The second movement follows the traditional structure of a scherzo and trio with the scherzo based in A minor, and the trio in the relative major of C. The main sections are as follows:

Scherzo

■   From beginning of movement to figure 57

Comprising:

■   Introduction: beginning up to figure 49
■   'A' section: figure 49 to 53
■   'B' section (first time): figure 53 to 55
■   'B' section (second time): figure 55 to 57

Trio

■   Figure 57 to figure 65

Comprising:

■   'A' section (first time): figure 57 to 59
■   'A' section (second time): figure 59 to 61
■   'B' section (first time): figure 61 to 63
■   'B' section (second time): figure 63 to 65

Scherzo

■   Figure 65 to end of movement (after figure 74)

Comprising:

■   Introduction: figure 65 to 66
■   'A' section: figure 66 to 69
■   'B' section (first time): figure 69 to 71
■   'B' section (second time): figure 71 to three bars after figure 73

Codetta

■   Three bars after figure 73 to end of movement

In the second movement, passages for which it would be advisable to have revision notes are:

■   Scherzo 'A' section: figure 49 to 53 – provided below

- Scherzo 'B' section: figure 53 to 57
- Trio 'A' section: figure 57 to 59
- Codetta: figure 73 to end of movement.

What follows is an example of a page of revision notes for the scherzo 'A' section to get you started.

EXAMPLE REVISION PAGE: SECOND MOVEMENT – SCHERZO 'A' SECTION (FIGURE 49 TO 53)

Structure: There is a 12-bar introduction to the movement. The main scherzo material starts at figure 49. There is a series of five phrases that are differentiated by scoring.

Melody: There are a number of different melodic ingredients. Important elements in the cello/bass introduction are the bar of repeating A quavers, and the following bar of scalic contour.

The Eb clarinet theme picks up on the scalic pattern before surprising the listener with more angular shapes before figure 50.

A phrase for the woodwinds at figure 50 utilises the repeating quavers idea.

The bassoon is next to take the melody and has more patterns, whereas subsequent violin melodies integrate these with the repeating quavers.

Rhythm: The triple time metre (traditional for a scherzo) gives the music a sense of dance (the tradition of Russian ballet seeming so far away) and the heavy reliance on quavers (often staccato) gives the music considerable momentum.

The accompaniment underlines the dance feel with frequent use of rests – either on the third beat of the bar (horns after figure 49) or on the downbeats (bass line four bars before figure 51).

Harmony/Tonality: The tonal sense is A minor, but in a modal way: Shostakovich avoids the leading note of G♯ and instead used B♭ to create a dark, Phrygian character.

The harmonic dimension is light and delicate. The opening Eb clarinet phrase just has touches of harmony in two parts on the horns, whereas the later bassoon phrase is accompanied by only a bass line (and one with rests in at that). Nonetheless, there are touches of chromaticism in Shostakovich's harmonic palette; for instance, four bars after figure 50 and also four bars after figure 52.

Texture: In the introduction the texture is a monophonic bass line.

Thereafter, the texture is dominated by the melodic line. The winds have a homophonic texture at figure 50; at figure 51 the texture is a counterpoint of the melody in the bassoon with the bass line that is the material that formed the introduction.

Orchestration:	This passage is a good illustration of Shostakovich's interest in exploring extreme and contrasting registers. The introduction is just the cellos and basses, whereas the opening melody is given primarily to the high-pitched small E♭ clarinet. Good use is also made of the upper register of the bassoon before figure 51.
Effect:	There is something of a *danse macabre* to this section: a devilish quality. It is brittle and sardonic.

THIRD MOVEMENT

This great elegiac movement is essentially a unique structure that uses four different ideas and builds from them a vast landscape in which emotional tension is always present, whether in a distilled intimate way or a great climax of almost brutal intensity.

The order of the four ideas (referred to here as A, B, C and D) is as follows:

- Start (figure 75): A
- Figure 78: B
- Figure 79: C
- Figure 81: A
- Figure 83: B
- Figure 84: D
- Figure 87: A
- Figure 89: B – the movement's great climax
- Figure 90: D
- Figure 93: A
- Figure 94: C
- Figure 96: D

In the third movement, passages for which it would be advisable to have revision notes are:

- The opening 'A' section: figure 75 to 78
- The first 'B' section: figure 78 to 79
- The first 'C' section: figure 79 to 81
- The first 'D' section: figure 84 to 87
- The climax: figure 89 to 93
- The ending: figure 96 to end of movement.

Below is an example of how the opening 'A' section might look:

EXAMPLE REVISION PAGE: THIRD MOVEMENT – OPENING 'A' SECTION (FIGURE 75 TO 78)

Structure:	This is essentially one long paragraph of string music with a slow-moving melodic line. Greater intensity is found after figure 77 through a wider and fuller texture (and louder dynamic).
Melody:	The melody is largely stepwise, but there are some leaps such as the 4ths in bars 1 and 3. The major 6th in the third bar after figure 76 sounds particularly yearning. The melody is almost entirely diatonic until figure

	77, after which considerably more chromaticism is used to intensify the musical effect.
Rhythm:	The rhythm is slow, with nothing faster than quavers used (at the largo tempo). The bass line is even more slowly moving until figure 77.
	The opening melodic line twice has a rhythmic unit of a three-beat note (that includes a tie) followed by a pair of quavers: a rhythmic augmentation of a significant motif in the first movement of dotted quaver and two demisemiquavers (e.g. bar 3 of the symphony's opening).
Harmony/Tonality:	F♯ minor is apparent as the tonic key from the start, though not confirmed by any sharpened leading notes. The harmony is only produced by three lines in the texture, and sometimes this leads to bare harmonies such as at figure 76 where an open 4th changes to an open 5th.
	From figure 77, the sense of key becomes obscured by some very chromatic writing, and there is a strange cadence that moves out onto an F♯ major chord at figure 78.
Texture:	Up as far as figure 77, there is a simple texture formed by three long legato strands: the melodic line in the third violins, a bass line on the second cellos and basses, and a countermelody in the first violas.
	A richer texture takes over at figure 77 with the melodic line doubled in 3rds in two violin parts, and both these lines in turn being doubled at a lower octave by the second violas and first cellos.
Orchestration:	Shostakovich solely depends on his string section for the opening to this movement. However, he divides it into more parts than is standard: three violin parts, two viola parts, two cello parts and the basses. This makes for a reduced sound as the movement begins.
	The movement will make no use of brass instruments at all.
Effect:	The music sounds profoundly sorrowful and introspective.

FOURTH MOVEMENT

Shostakovich writes a unique structure that is focused on the culmination of the symphony at figure 131. There is a sense of a tri-partite shape:

First section: Figure 97 to 111. Two themes stand out:

- The opening march idea in D minor heard right at the start
- The exuberant disjunct melody at figure 110 in A major.

Second section: Figure 111 to 121. This comprises some thematic transformation but is largely concerned with other material and is largely based in B♭.

Third section: Figure 121 to 134. A lengthy dominant pedal underpins the return to D minor. There is a long build up using material from the first section, though there is little room for the exuberant second theme. The culmination of the movement is reached at figure 131 with a (compromised) sense of D major.

In the finale, passages for which it would be advisable to have revision notes are:

- First section: from the opening up to figure 102
- First section: the build-up from figure 107 to 110
- First section: the celebratory anthem from figure 110 to 111
- Second section: the recollection of the celebratory theme: figure 112 to 113
- Second section: the withdrawn quiet passage: figure 116 to 121
- Third section: the start of the build-up: figure 121 to 124
- Third section: the last part of the build-up: figure 128 to 131
- Third section: the culmination: figure 131 to end of movement.

Here is an example of how the revision page for the final passage might look.

EXAMPLE REVISION PAGE: FOURTH MOVEMENT – THIRD SECTION: THE CULMINATION (FIGURE 131 TO THE END OF THE MOVEMENT)

Structure:	Late in the symphony the music reaches D major and this conclusion is built around the finale's march theme now converted (by rhythmic augmentation and the change to the major) into an anthem played in stentorian tones on the brass.
	There is a clear phrase structure to the brass chorale, and from figure 134 the brass section hammers out the tonic chord.
	Meanwhile, through the passage almost the whole of the rest of the orchestra are declaiming the note A in an industrial repetitive manner.
Melody:	The brass anthem is a variant of the opening theme to the movement, now with all of the leaps, save for the anacrusis dominant to tonic, reduced to conjunct motion.
Rhythm:	The use of rhythmic augmentation now has the melody in minims and crotchets with even longer notes after figure 133.
	The insistent As played by strings and winds are continuous in relentless quavers.
Harmony/Tonality:	Initially it might seem that this is going to be an unreservedly triumphant and joyous conclusion in D major.
	However, the harmonic vocabulary does not have that sense of freedom and conviction. There are no strong dominant 7th harmonies to reinforce the key, and when the chord tries, eventually, to change (at figure 132), it is to a minor IV chord that clashes with the insistent As in the strings and wind (B♭ against A).
Texture:	There are essentially just two elements to the texture here: the homophonic brass anthem and the intense dominant inverted pedal. The timpani and percussion add a further element of colour.
Orchestration:	The scoring in this final passage is relatively straightforward. The brass carry the main substance, with trumpets right at the top of their range. Almost all other instruments are playing quaver As, with consideration

given to the challenge of this to the E♭ clarinettist who is given a concession to play crotchets. The timpani and percussion are very effective with the D–A patterns on the timpani and the cymbal clashes and triangle rolls all adding vivid colour. Towards the end the snare drum adds a further intensity, and then in the final bars the bass drum, marked *fff*, completes the overwhelming intensity.

Effect: The end of this symphony is famously open to various interpretations. The sheer intensity of the music and drive is mighty and can be overwhelming. However, the context in which the symphony was written in 1937 Soviet Russia makes the message uncertain: is it a triumphant hymn to Stalin and the communist machine, or a resilient and defiant protest that expresses solidarity with the people? Or is it, at a more personal level, a statement of an individual's struggle and ultimate self-belief?

WHOLE SYMPHONY ASPECTS

It is harder to predict what angles the examiners might choose for a second question that looks at the whole symphony as there is no clear limit to how imaginatively they might think. Part of the skill on your part, and something for which the examiners will give credit, is being able to 'think on your feet' and draw on your knowledge to fit the question. However, you will be best prepared to do this if you have considered at least some of the possible angles. Here is a list of suggestions:

- Ways in which the musical language is clearly of the 20th century
- Examples of Shostakovich's innovative and distinctive orchestration
- The importance of tonal centres through the symphony
- Examples of rhythmic diminution and augmentation in the symphony
- Passages that show the emotional range of the symphony
- Reasons for the symphony's popularity.

When compiling your revision notes for these topics, it is important to avoid writing down everything that might be relevant. Each question could be answered by at least a whole chapter of a book, and you only have 50 minutes to write in the exam. Instead, think of how you will structure the essay and only choose the best examples: examples that you can remember easily.

What follows is an example of how a revision page for the first of these topics might look.

EXAMPLE REVISION PAGE: WHOLE SYMPHONY TOPIC – 20TH-CENTURY ASPECTS

Structure: Although Shostakovich structures his symphony in the traditional four-movement plan, his approach to sonata form in the outer movements shows much more freedom and innovation than is usually found in the Romantic era.

In the first movement, the exposition lacks the clear structure of first subject – transition – second subject – codetta.

- The first subject is almost immediately developmental, with conflicting ideas adapted and combined (e.g. the introductory idea quickly transforms into an accompaniment pattern at figure 1; at figure 6 the introductory idea is a counterpoint to the violin tune from before figure 4, which is now heard in the bass).
- Tonal centres are less stable: as early as bar 13, the opening music is heard a tone lower in C minor.
- The key relationship of the second subject at figure 9 is neither the dominant nor the relative major. Instead we go from the home key of D minor to Eb minor.
- The second subject idea later returns in B minor (figure 15) where we might expect the codetta.

This approach makes for a long development. However, the really innovative section is the recapitulation. Shostakovich does not give us the main first subject theme when the recap starts (at figure 36); instead he uses material from either side of figure 4 which seemed to be subsidiary in the exposition, and he does so with overwhelming force. The main first subject finally appears where one would usually find a coda (figure 44), and it is inverted.

The second movement, the scherzo and trio, is a more standard structure. Both the third and fourth movements, however, are original structures that are specific to the emotional needs of each movement.

- The third movement uses four separate ideas in a varied order, building to an intense climax using the second of these ideas at figure 89.
- The finale (in D minor) has something approaching a standard sonata form exposition, with an exuberant second subject in the dominant major at figure 110. The exposition, however, follows a different course. Beginning at figure 121 over a dominant pedal, there is a lengthy build-up until the tonic major is eventually reached at figure 131, but here it is the first subject that is used to finish the symphony; the second subject has not been used again.

Melody:

Shostakovich's melodic ideas in this symphony are diverse, and include:

- The jagged, angular contour of the first two bars of the symphony
- The use of Phrygian mode at figure 1
- The second phrase of the first subject at figure 1 which uses all 12 tones of the scale
- The very wide-leaping second subject in the first movement (figure 9)
- Melodies that can pass through various tonal centres, for example the flute entry either side of figure 14 (which starts in F# minor and ends suggesting Eb major)
- Melodies that include glissandos, such as in the trio section of the second movement (figure 57)
- Long, wandering melodies such as the one that starts the third movement

- Short snatches of melody, such as the idea used at the third movement climax at figure 89
- The largely disjunct second subject in the finale at figure 110, which consists of many 4ths (including one augmented 4th).

Rhythm:

After the incisive rhythms of the opening two bars, most of the symphony is fairly conventional in rhythmic terms.

However, the driving, mechanistic rhythms that feature in several places during the outer movements (e.g. figure 27 to 32 in the first movement, and from figure 126 in the finale) do seem to suggest the century of industrialised mass production and totalitarianism.

Harmony/Tonality:

The symphony makes use of some unusual key relationships, such as the move from D minor to E♭ minor for the second subject in the first movement.

This sense of harmonic instability is distinctly of the 20th century. For example, no sooner has D minor been established at figure 1 than additional chromatic notes are brought into both the melody and the harmony. The chord progression underpinning the second subject (figure 10) is also far from a standard diatonic functional harmony.

Shostakovich freely uses dissonant harmony when he requires it. The first climax of the symphony at figure 8 has a searing dissonance with F♮ and F♯ in a chord that is played nine times. The *fff* timpani tritone that is sounded for six bars at figure 111 in the finale is another very 20th-century effect, particularly as the timpani are used to dominate the orchestral canvas at this point.

Texture:

From the moment the symphony starts in canon, there is clarity to the textures that avoid romantic luxuriousness and are instead often sparse and widely spaced.

Good examples are:

- The first subject floating in high above the viola/cello accompaniment at figure 1
- A similar effect at figure 9 with the second subject
- The unusual three-part texture at figure 12 for *divisi* violas where one part is in a high register and the other – in dialogue with the cellos – is low on the C-string
- The extraordinary texture at the first movement recapitulation with just a melodic line played *fff* in four octaves
- The 'C' idea of the third movement at figure 79 with two flutes – one high up, the other in low register – accompanied just by an ostinato harp pattern
- The climax of the third movement at figure 89 with the melody hammered out in third octaves (all at the upper half of register) with a similarly high tremolo chord.

Orchestration:	Shostakovich calls for a few instruments which are more likely to be found in 20th-century orchestral music: the E♭ clarinet, the xylophone, the celesta and the piano.
	It is in the use of the instruments, however, and not simply the choice, that he shows his distinctive 20th-century ethos, with each instrument used for its own colour and not often just as a member of the string, wind or brass section as a whole. This leads to some exotic combinations of instruments. He also seems fascinated by the particular timbres available when instruments play at the extremes of their compass. Good examples to cite include:

- The bassoons in octaves at figure 2 doubled by pizzicato low strings
- *Divisi* violas at figure 12 exploiting the distinctive timbres of the instrument in both high and low registers simultaneously
- Use of piano with pizzicato cellos and basses in the low register to start the development at figure 17 followed by an entry for all four horns in unison at the bottom of their range
- The insistent xylophone from the third bar of figure 29
- The duet for flute and horn from figure 39
- The piccolo solo after figure 45
- The celesta chromatic scales at the end of the first movement
- The E♭ clarinet solo early in the second movement (figure 49)
- The unaccompanied melody in octaves for bassoon and contrabassoon at figure 65
- The unusual division of the strings into eight sections for the third movement
- The tremolo chord – especially on the piano at the third movement climax at figure 89
- The scoring at figure 91 with high cellos (doubled by upper winds) and low tremolo violas and clarinets.

Ten particularly good passages to use for illustrating 20th-century aspects of Shostakovich's musical language are:

First movement

- The main first subject at figure 1: modal and then all 12 tones
- The second subject at figure 9: an unusual key relationship, wide-ranging melodic contour and colourful harmonic palette
- The recapitulation at figure 36: structurally daring by not starting with first subject, extraordinary scoring and texture.

Second movement

- The first scherzo melody at figure 49: a seven-bar phrase of diverse contours, played by the E♭ clarinet
- The start of the trio at figure 57: solo violin melody with glissandos, accompanied by harp.

Third movement

- The final part of the opening 'A' section at figure 77: eight-part division of string section, extreme chromaticism in melody and harmony within F♯ minor context, unusual cadence into figure 78
- The climax of the movement at figure 89: originality of scoring and texture, especially with regard to piano and xylophone.

Fourth movement

- The second idea in the opening march theme at figure 98. This is initially a diatonic melody that then gains extra chromatic pitches around figure 99; its high register is scored with two flutes and E♭ clarinet doubling the upper violin line; the horn entry is distinctly aggressive
- The start to the second section at figure 111: a tritone hammered out on the timpani, use of tam-tam, powerful entry for trombones and tuba followed by a frenzied bar for the full orchestra (the lowest two parts climb chromatically in tritones)
- The molto ritenuto into figure 131: starts with only very high register, thrilling dissonant brass chords fill in underneath as the symphony finally makes it to D major.

Writing essays – accessing the marks

Mark schemes for previous Unit 4 papers are available on the AQA website.

Your essays will be assessed for the following qualities:

- Knowledge and understanding of the music
- Relevance to the question set
- Points supported by reference to the score
- Confident use of specialist vocabulary
- Structure of the argument in your essay
- Writing style.

Bearing these factors in mind, you can see that you want to avoid the following pitfalls:

- Factual inaccuracies and incorrect analytical comment
- Writing about aspects of the music that are not relevant to the question
- Making general points that are not backed up by specific references to the score
- Not using appropriate technical terms, or using technical vocabulary in inaccurate ways
- Starting your essay without a clear sense of the argument you want to make in answer to the question, or spending too long making one point so that you do not have time to make others with equal weight
- Writing with poor spelling or grammar.

Writing good music essays requires practice. In particular:

- The more you have studied the symphony, the more your analytical understanding will be accurate and comprehensive.
- The more angles from whch you have considered each movement, the quicker you will locate the best examples that will support the points you make. (Remember: you will not have your own personal copy of the score in the exam room with your annotations in it.)

- The more you use specialist vocabulary in conversation, reading about music, making revision notes and writing about the symphony, the more comfortable and convincing you will be in using technical terms in the exam room.
- The more practice essays you write, the better your writing style will be, and the more confident you will be, helping you to keep to time in the exam.

Therefore, make sure you factor into your revision schedule times when you will practise writing essays.

Above all, it is important to convince the examiners that you can hear the effect of the music you are writing about – as though you have a private performance playing in an earpiece in the exam room. This is much more impressive than just describing what you can see on the page in the score.

TWO PARAGRAPHS TO CONSIDER

Now imagine you are an examiner and you are marking two attempts to answer the following question:

Write a detailed account of Shostakovich's fifth symphony. You should refer to structure, melody, rhythm and tonality.

Candidate A's answer begins like this:

> The second movement begins in C major with the cellos and basses in unison. The main tune comes in at figure 49 with the flute and piccolo in 3rds accompanied by horns. There are some trills early on to decorate the tune. Once the flute drops out the music becomes piano and more gentle, until some louder music at figure 50. After figure 51 the strings take over the music from the wind section, however they play similar melodies until a new tune enters on the winds at figure 53. This tune has lots of rests in it as well as some long notes for the trumpet. The percussion also start to play here.

Candidate B's answer begins this way:

> The second movement is essentially a traditional scherzo and trio in ternary form where the outer sections are in A minor and the trio is in the relative major. The scherzo section has a short introduction for cellos and basses in octaves, and then two halves, the second of which has a written out, re-scored repeat. The two halves contrast both in rhythm - the first half is largely quavers, whereas the second (figure 53) has, effectively crisp dotted rhythms - and also in tonality, the second half beginning in C minor. The main characteristics in the melody of the first half are scalic patterns (apparent from figure 49), and repeating quavers, especially when the violin take the melodic line after figure 51. There are also two bars of disjunct motion in the Eb clarinet tune before figure 50 which adds to the spiky, quirky scherzo mood.

Which of these seem like the candidate is on the way to a high mark? If you realised it was the second then you are correct. Here there is a clear addressing of the question (structure, melody, rhythm and tonality), successful use of technical vocabulary, careful referencing to examples in the score by bar number, and comment on the resulting sound of the details mentioned. Better still, have you noticed that the candidate has already created a guide to what else is to come in the essay, by stating simply the structural basis of the movement?

Candidate A has not made a promising start. Have you noticed all the reasons why not? We do not yet know what form the candidate thinks the music is in; there are some factual errors concerning the key of the movement (the lack of key signature does not mean C major!) and understanding the instrumentation (the melody is not on the piccolo by the E♭ clarinet which needs to be transposed – the tune is not in 3rds with the flute!); attention is needlessly being given to instrumentation which is not in the question; rhythm and melodic contour are only referred to in general terms, without technical vocabulary or referencing examples in the score, and the attempt to describe the resulting sound ('gentle') strongly suggests that the candidate cannot recall what the music actually sounds like.

There are lots of good warnings here to take heed of in order to ensure you do not fall into the same traps.

Unit 4 – Section C: Historical Study – Area of Study 3 (selected topic)

The final section of the Unit 4 exam is based on your selected historical topic. You will have been learning about music from one of the following topics:

- English Choral Music in the 20th century
- Chamber Music from Mendelssohn to Debussy
- Four Decades of Jazz and Blues 1910–1950.

For each of these topics there will be two essay titles on the exam paper, and you only have to answer **one** question from the topic you have been studying. You should have about 50 minutes in the exam to answer the question you have chosen.

In part, this is a similar challenge to the one met in Section B: a test of your ability to write well on the music you have been studying, giving good analytical detail, making use of appropriate technical vocabulary and in a way that is clearly relevant to the question you are answering.

However, there is an extra dimension here. In Section B, where all candidates have been studying the same piece, you are allowed a copy of the score with you in the exam room; in Section C, where there are no set works and so you and your teacher have had the opportunity to select your own choice of music representative of the topic, you are not allowed to take scores into the exam. This means that Section C is also a test of your musical memory. Without the visual aid of a score to turn to, you will need to be able to recall the sound of the music in your inner ear unprompted. It is therefore very important that you factor into your revision timetable plenty of opportunity for listening to the music you have been studying in this area.

Across the country, a wide range of music will have been studied for these three topics, so it is not possible for a book of this scope to cover every piece that you may have been looking at for your selected topic. You will need to refer to your own notes – and any textbook you have been using through the course such as the Rhinegold *Study Guide* – to remind yourself of the important facts and analysis that you have covered.

What you will find below is some advice for each topic on how to prepare your revision notes for this section and how to make sure you have covered a wide enough range of music for your chosen topic.

Writing essays – accessing the marks

The marking of Section C essays is very similar to Section B. Examiners will be looking for the following strengths in your essay:

- Sound knowledge and understanding of the music
- Clear relevance to the question set

- Specific points supported by references to the music you have studied, maybe giving some musical quotes
- Correct and confident use of specialist vocabulary
- Structure of the argument in your essay
- An awareness of context
- A mature writing style.

If you have been working on chamber music, turn to page 65. If you have chosen jazz and blues, turn to page 67. The section on English 20th-century choral music follows on straight away.

Area of Study 3a: English Choral Music in the 20th century

You need to be prepared for questions that can come from the following angles:

- Type of writing for voices: solo passages, choral writing
  Example: *Choose two contrasting passages of choral writing from the music you have studied, and explain how the composers have been effective in handling the text and the choral forces.*
- Different emotional moods
  Example: *Choose two passages of music by different composers that create contrasting emotions and explain how the composers have achieved this.*
- Change in musical language over time
  Example: *Choose two works from different decades of the 20th century that you have studied and highlight some of the differences in musical language between the two.*
- Different composers
  Example: *Assess the contribution of one of the following, highlighting aspects of the way they wrote for voices.*
  - Elgar
  - Britten
  - Rutter
  - Jenkins
- Practical issues: performing the music
  Example: *In what ways does choral music since 1945 provide new challenges to the singers?*

In most of these cases, the examiners might steer you to consider certain elements of music from the following list: structure, melody, rhythm, harmony and tonality, texture and use of voices.

Bearing all these aspects in mind, it would be a good idea to organise your revision notes for this section in a methodical manner so that you have a systematic approach to learning information about different pieces that might combine to answer one of these questions.

Use a separate piece of paper for each passage of music you have studied, and organise it in a way that will allow you to separate out all the different elements. For example:

Passage of music	
Composer/date	
Emotion/mood	
Structure	
Melodic detail	
Tonality/harmonic detail	
Rhythmic detail	
Textures	
Use of voices/word setting	

With the information organised this way, when you are writing a practice essay you can have the relevant pages to hand that suit just that essay, and – if the question specifies only certain elements of music – refer to those sections of each page of your revision notes.

TOP TEN TIPS FOR WRITING ABOUT ENGLISH CHORAL MUSIC

- Plan your essay.
- Structure your essay in paragraphs. Leave a line between paragraphs – it makes the text easier to read, makes you think with greater clarity and gives you space to add an afterthought.
- Make sure you have an argument that answers the question.
- If certain elements of music have been set, make sure you focus on them.
- Make sure that the points you make in your argument are supported by specific examples found in the music you have studied.
- Identify precisely the location of your example; this is probably best done by citing the text at this point.
- Use technical vocabulary to discuss the musical point.
- If you have time, write out a short fragment of the music on the manuscript paper.
- Describe briefly the resulting sound of the music you have used to support your argument.
- Be aware of the context of the music you are writing about, but refer to it only in passing. Long descriptions of context will not gain you credit and use up valuable time; brief references show you understand the significance of the context.

Area of Study 3b: Chamber Music from Mendelssohn to Debussy

You need to be prepared for questions that can come from the following angles:

- Different scorings
  Example: *Choose two pieces, one for three or four players, the other for five or more. How is the greater number of players reflected in the approach to texture?*
- Different emotional moods
  Example: *Choose two movements by different composers that create contrasting emotions and explain how the composers have achieved this.*
- Change in musical language over time
  Example: *Choose two movements from different decades of the 19th century that you have studied and highlight some of the differences in musical language between the two.*
- Different composers
  Example: *Assess the contribution of one of the following, highlighting their approach to instrumental writing.*
  - Mendelssohn
  - Schumann
  - Dvořák
  - Tchaikovsky
  - Debussy
- Practical issues: performing the music
  Example: *Choose a chamber work you have studied and discuss the challenges presented to the players in interpreting and performing the music.*

In most of these cases, the examiners might steer you to consider certain elements of music from the following list: structure, melody, rhythm, harmony and tonality, texture and use of instruments.

Bearing all these aspects in mind, it would be a good idea to organise your revision notes for this section in a methodical manner so that you have a systematic approach to learning information about different pieces that might combine to answer one of these questions.

Use a separate piece of paper for each movement you have studied, and organise it in a way that will allow you to separate out all the different elements. For example:

Movement/work	
Composer/date	
Instrumentation	
Emotion/mood	
Structure	
Melodic detail	
Tonality/harmonic detail	
Rhythmic detail	
Textures	
Use of instruments	

With the information organised this way, when you are writing a practice essay you can have the relevant pages to hand that suit just that essay, and – if the question specifies only certain elements of music – refer to those sections of each page of your revision notes.

TOP TEN TIPS FOR WRITING ABOUT CHAMBER MUSIC

- Plan your essay.
- Structure your essay in paragraphs. Leave a line between paragraphs – it makes the text easier to read, makes you think with greater clarity and gives you space to add an afterthought.
- Make sure you have an argument that answers the question.
- If certain elements of music have been set, make sure you focus on them.
- Make sure that the points you make in your argument are supported by specific examples found in the music you have studied.
- Identify precisely the location of your example; this is probably best done by citing the text at this point.
- Use technical vocabulary to discuss the musical point.
- If you have time, write out a short fragment of the music on the manuscript paper.
- Describe briefly the resulting sound of the music you have used to support your argument.
- Be aware of the context of the music you are writing about, but refer to it only in passing. Long descriptions of context will not gain you credit and use up valuable time; brief references show you understand the significance of the context.

Area of Study 3c: Four Decades of Jazz and Blues 1910 to 1950

You need to be prepared for questions that can come from the following angles:

- Different musicians
  Example: *Assess the contribution of one of the following musicians:*
  - Louis Armstrong
  - Benny Goodman
  - Count Basie
  - Dizzy Gillespie
- Different styles
  Example: *Explain the differences in musical language and style between two of the following:*
  - Blues
  - Swing
  - Big band
  - Bebop
- Change in musical language over time
  Example: *Write an essay that shows how jazz developed between 1930 and 1950.*
- Different emotional moods
  Example: *Choose two jazz numbers by different musicians that create contrasting emotions and explain how they achieved this.*
- The influence on 'classical' composers
  Example: *Discuss at least two works of the classical repertoire that were the result of composers being influenced by developments in jazz and highlight the ways in which the influence can be heard.*
- In most of these cases, the examiners might steer you to consider certain elements of music from the following list: structure, melody, rhythm, harmony and tonality, texture and use of instruments.

Bearing all these aspects in mind, it would be a good idea to organise your revision notes for this section in a methodical manner so that you have a systematic approach to learning information about different pieces that might combine to answer one of these questions.

Use a separate piece of paper for each movement you have studied, and organise it in a way that will allow you to separate out all the different elements. For example:

Title of piece	
Artist/date	
Emotion/mood	
Structure	
Melodic detail	
Tonality/harmonic detail	
Rhythmic detail	
Textures	
Use of instruments	

With the information organised this way, when you are writing a practice essay you can have the relevant pages to hand that suit just that essay, and – if the question specifies only certain elements of music – refer to those sections of each page of your revision notes.

TOP TEN TIPS FOR WRITING ABOUT JAZZ AND BLUES

- Plan your essay.
- Structure your essay in paragraphs. Leave a line between paragraphs – it makes the text easier to read, makes you think with greater clarity and gives you space to add an afterthought.
- Make sure you have an argument that answers the question.
- If certain elements of music have been set, make sure you focus on them.
- Make sure that the points you make in your argument are supported by specific examples found in the music you have studied.
- Identify precisely the location of your example; this is probably best done by citing the text at this point.
- Use technical vocabulary to discuss the musical point.
- If you have time, write out a short fragment of the music on the manuscript paper.
- Describe briefly the resulting sound of the music you have used to support your argument.
- Be aware of the context of the music you are writing about, but refer to it only in passing. Long descriptions of context will not gain you credit and use up valuable time; brief references show you understand the significance of the context.

Unit 5 – Developing Musical Ideas

For Unit 5 you have to write music to one of three briefs:

- Brief A: Compositional Techniques
- Brief B: Free Composition or Pastiche
- Brief C: Arranging.

Details about what exactly is required in each year are published in the Developing Musical Ideas paper, which is available via the AQA website from 1 November. In all you have 20 hours of **controlled time** in which to complete one of the three briefs. Your teacher will discuss with you when these might best fit in with the school schedule and your own needs. Your work has to be submitted by 15 May (so you might even start on your submission as late as March) and needs to comprise:

- A score or annotation of the music you have composed
- A recording of the piece(s) you are submitting
- Your **Review** – see below
- The Candidate Record Form, which you must sign.

The score or annotation can be written by hand or printed from a computer. If you are answering Brief A, you may write your answer on the actual question paper (but you do not have to do it this way). Note that Brief A comprises two questions.

The recording may be an acoustic one of musicians performing your music or one of a computer playback. It is an important aid to the examiner but not part of the actual assessment. The recording can be made after the 20 hours of controlled time have passed.

The **Review** is a piece of writing in which you explain how you went about your work and is another significant guide to the examiner, so, although there are no marks specifically for it, it is worth spending time writing a good guide to your piece(s). You should cover aspects such as how you structured the music, what keys you used and how you sought to develop your ideas. Do not write more than 500 words. You may do this after the end of controlled time.

As this unit is more like coursework than an exam, there is no real revision required and it lies outside the main focus of this book. However, for each brief, there follows a checklist that you could use as you are getting ready to finish your work and prepare it for submission to the examiners.

> **NOTE**
>
> You will not be allowed to take this book into the room where you are completing your Unit 5 work under controlled time, but you can refer to it between sessions and remind yourself of important aspects that you wish to check just before you start a controlled time session.

Brief A – question 1

Checklist:

- Do you know what key the melody is in?
- Have you found a good range of modulations for the various phrases, considering all available related keys?
- Have you finished each phrase with a suitable cadence in the right place?
- Have you used a mix of root position and first-inversion chords?
- Are all diminished chords (VII in major keys, II and VII in minor keys) in first inversion?
- Are second-inversion chords only used in correct passing and cadential patterns?
- Have you put in all necessary accidentals where the music modulates?
- Have you found opportunity for some secondary 7th chords? (If not, consider each chord you have written and see if there is an opportunity to precede it with its own dominant 7th, carefully considering which inversion to use by looking at the bass line.)
- Have you used a V⁷d–Ib progression? (If not, look for a V–I progression that could be a secondary 7th, and see if you can change the inversions.)
- Have you used a diminished 7th chord anywhere? (If not, look for dominant 7th chords and see if you can raise its root note by a semitone.)
- Whenever you have a 7th in a chord, does it fall by step on the next beat?
- Does each voice part sit in an appropriate register?
- Are the A, T and B parts easy to sing, avoiding intervals such as augmented 2nds?
- Have you found opportunities for passing notes in the lower parts?
- Do your passing notes always move by step?
- Have you checked every pair of parts to make sure there are no parallel 5ths or octaves? (Check S/A, S/T, S/B, A/T, A/B and T/B.)
- Does your Review explain which keys you have modulated to and what cadences you have used?

Brief A – question 2

Checklist:

- Have you copied the given part accurately and not altered it all (perhaps by accident) whilst completing the task?
- Have you considered the structure of the given material and found where cadences are required?
- Have you considered the key of the music and found any modulations to related keys that are implied?
- Have you found opportunity to vary the texture, making use of some rests in the lower parts at times?
- Have you found opportunity for some chromatic harmony? (If not, find a significant dominant chord and see if you can work an augmented 6th chord on the preceding beat. This will be formed on the flattened 6th degree of the scale.)

- Have you followed **to the letter** the instructions for filling in the blank bars, using the suggested material while varying it a little (you might try it in the bass, at a different octave, with an altered harmonisation or even in the tonic minor)?
- If you have used specialist string techniques such as double-stopping or pizzicato, are they really effective and used with restraint?
- Have you checked that there are no parallel 5ths between any parts, especially between the first violin and cello?
- Have you taken care to edit the score with dynamic and bowing markings for the lower three parts?
- Does your Review explain how you set about the task, which keys you modulate to, how you created some variety in the texture and how you used the suggested material to fill the blank bars?

Brief B

Checklist:

- Does your piece last five to eight minutes?
- Is there a clear and effective structure?
- If you have composed two or three shorter movements, is there a clear connection between them to form one strong piece?
- Is there some contrast of tonality?
- Is there a good rhythmic character to your piece?
- Are the melodic ideas well shaped and memorable?
- Have you developed your material and not just relied on simple repetition?
- If your piece involves singing, does the text fit the melodic line convincingly?
- Have you created interest in your harmonic writing (for example: primary *and* secondary chords, a variety of inversions, chromatic inflections such as secondary 7ths or the Neapolitan 6th, modulation, changing harmonic rhythm, pedal notes)?
- Is there something imaginative and varied in your handling of texture? For instance, have you explored contrasts in register, invented a variety of patterns in the accompaniment, tried doubling a melodic line in octaves or put the melody in the bass or tenor register? Have you made use of rests as well as notes?
- Have you considered the changes of timbre that your chosen instruments offer? Have you varied the dynamic and articulation?
- If you are providing a score, is it clearly edited and well formatted (with a sensible number or bars per page)?
- If you are providing an annotation, does it set out clearly the structure and musical content of your piece in a way that will communicate your creative ideas directly to the examiner?
- Does your Review shed light on decisions you took during the composing process on how the piece was to be structured and how you were going to create musical character and contrast in your piece?

Brief C

Checklist:

- Does your piece last five to eight minutes?
- Is there a clear and effective structure?
- Is it clearly based on the set material? Have you looked at including melodic, rhythmic and harmonic elements of the original in your arrangement? Have you considered the potential of all sections of the set piece?
- Have you used a recognisable jazz, rock or pop style for your arrangement?
- Is there some contrast of tonality?
- Is there a clear rhythmic character to your piece?
- Are the melodic ideas well shaped and memorable?
- Have you developed your material and not just relied on simple repetition?
- Have you created interest in your harmonic writing (for example: primary **and** secondary chords, a variety of inversions, chromatic inflections, modulation, changing harmonic rhythm, pedal notes)?
- Is there something imaginative and varied in your handling of texture? For instance, have you explored contrasts in register, invented a variety of patterns in the accompaniment, tried doubling a melodic line in octaves or put the melody in the bass or tenor register? Have you made use of rests as well as notes?
- Have you considered the changes of timbre that your chosen instruments offer? Have you varied the dynamic and articulation? If you have used a drum kit, have you incorporated a variety of rhythmic patterns, timbres, dynamics and passages where the drummer does not play?
- If you are providing a score, is it clearly edited and well formatted (with a sensible number or bars per page)?
- If you are providing an annotation, does it set out clearly the structure and musical content of your piece in a way that will communicate your creative ideas directly to the examiner?
- Does your Review shed light on decisions you took during the composing process on how you used the set piece, what elements you took from it and how you developed and structured your own piece in response to it?

Unit 6 – A Musical Performance

For Unit 6 you need to choose one of the following routes:

- A solo acoustic performance lasting 10–15 minutes
- Two technology-based performances: sequencing and multi-track/close microphone project
- One solo acoustic performance of five minutes and one of the technology options.

Details of what is involved for each option are available in the AQA specification. You can complete your chosen option at any point during the A2 course. Your work needs to be submitted to an AQA examiner by 15 May. Your submission will need to comprise:

- The recording relevant to your option
- Supporting material such as scores of your performance, original material for the piece you have sequenced, etc.
- The Candidate Record Form, which you must sign.

As this unit is more like coursework than an exam, there is no real revision required and it lies outside the main focus of this book. However, some checklists are provided here that you could use as you are getting ready to complete this unit, so that your submission makes a favourable impression on your examiner.

Solo acoustic performance

Checklist:

- Is your performance 10–15 minutes in duration?
- Does the 10–15 minutes feature largely your playing, or is there a long introduction?
- And is that 10–15 minutes without relying on repeats of the same music played the same way?
- Are you playing the music accurately?

> **NOTE**
>
> If your performance is not accurate, it is likely to lose marks for accuracy, communication and interpretation. Generally, it is **much** better to play music you find technically comfortable and can therefore communicate and interpret confidently than trying to play music you think is more technically impressive. This is true even if it costs you a mark or two for level of difficulty: you will more than make them up elsewhere in the mark scheme.

- Are you performing the music at the correct tempo?
- Have you given each piece a well-shaped interpretation with a good dynamic range, consideration of articulation, appropriate use of *rubato* or tempo changes, and a general awareness of the style of the music?
- Are you confident in the manner in which you are performing the music?
- Have you (or your teacher possibly) listened to the recording? If you can perform the music more accurately, or with a stronger sense of interpretation or communication, it will pay to do another take (though this will also depend on how hard you have practised in advance).
- Is the quality of the recording good?

Technology I: Sequencing

Checklist:

- Is your piece at least 48 bars long?
- Are there at least six instrumental or vocal parts?
- If it is in a 'classical' style, is there a solo part?
- If it is in a pop or jazz style, is there a vocal part?
- Have you controlled pitch and rhythm accurately?
- Is the performance at an appropriate tempo?
- Have you paid close attention to the expressive detail in terms of controlling timbre, dynamic, attack and issues such as balance and panning?
- Have you shown a clear appreciation of the style of the music?
- Is the final recording well balanced?

Technology 2: Multi-track or close microphone recording

Checklist:

- Is the piece at least 48 bars long?
- Are there at least six independent vocal and instrumental lines?
- Have you performed at least one of the parts?
- Have you used effects such as reverb and delay, and also considered the stereo field?
- Is there a good dynamic range?
- Does the recording have a good balance?

Answers for Unit 4 – Section A: Listening

Answers and comments on exercises

EXERCISE 1 (PAGE 13)

The music for the piece you have just heard is:

Answers

You should therefore have ticked the chart to show diminished 7th chords on the following beats:

2^2, 3^2, 4^2, 6^1, 7^1, 7^2, 10^2

The music for the piece you have just heard is:

Answers

a. The following bars have augmented 6th chords: 4, 8 and 12
b. The time signature is $\begin{smallmatrix}6\\8\end{smallmatrix}$
c. Duplet quavers
d. Plagal cadence.

Comments

■ Like most augmented 6th chords, the three examples here resolve out onto a 6/4 chord. The one in bar 8 takes the music briefly to the relative minor (A minor).

■ Although you are told that the music is 'in 2' in the question, the time signature has to be $\frac{6}{8}$ because the beat is subdivided into three: the hallmark of compound time.

■ In the middle of the piece there are a few beats in which the beat is subdivided into two. Given the compound metre, this is called duplet subdivision: the opposite of triplets in simple time.

■ The final cadence is plagal (IV → V): it produces a sense of finality, but the tonic note is present in both chords, unlike in a perfect cadence (V → I).

EXERCISE 3 (PAGE 13)

The music for the piece you have just heard is:

Answers

a. Secondary 7th chords are heard at bar 2², 4², 5², 7¹ and 8¹

b. The secondary 7th that takes the music flatwards is at bar 5², which is chord V of IV

c. Bars 3–4 are a rising sequence of bars 1–2 both melodically and harmonically

d. The cadence in bars 3–4 is imperfect (IIb → V)

e. The cadence in bars 9–10 is perfect (V⁷ → I).

Comments

■ The secondary 7th chords here account for all the chromatic (='colourful') moments in the piece and, as such, stand out to the listener (note: not the hearer). The melody is purely diatonic; colour is provided by the harmony.

■ Of the available secondary 7th chords (V of II, V of III, V of IV, V of V and V of VI – all of which occur in this piece), only V of IV includes a 'flat' coloured chord.

EXERCISE 4 (PAGE 14)

The music for the piece you have just heard is:

Answers

a. Dominant 7th chords in third inversion are heard at bars 0^3, 1^2, 2^3, 3^2, 4^3, 5^2, 6^{1-3}, 8^3 and 10^3

b. Most of these are secondary 7th chords:
- Bar 1^2 is V^7d of IV
- Bar 2^3 is V^7d of II
- Bar 3^2 is V^7d of V
- Bar 5^2 is V^7d of VI
- Bar 6^{1-3} is V^7d of IV
- Bar 8^3 is V^7d of III.

c. Bars 3–4 are a rising sequence of bars 1–2 (both melodically and harmonically)

d. A dominant pedal is used at bar 9^1 to 10^2.

Comments

- Note how all appearances of a dominant 7th chord in third inversion (V^7d) move onto the first inversion of the corresponding tonic.
- The dominant note in the bass at bar 9 to 10 underpins five beats of shifting harmony above, thus making this a pedal note.

EXERCISE 5 (PAGE 14)

The music for the piece you have just heard is:

Answers

a. Dominant 7th chords in third inversion are heard at bar 1³ and bar 2⁴

b. The chord at bar 2⁴ is a secondary 7th – V⁷d of VI

c. Half close cadences are heard in bars 4 and 8

d. The chord at bar 6 is not a secondary 7th, being chord Vd in the home key of C major. The chord at bar 5¹ is V⁷d of II, and the chord at bar 7³ is V⁷b of V

e. There is an augmented 6th chord in bar 11, lasting the entire bar. It does the usual progression of moving to Ic

f. The cadence at bars 15–16 is an interrupted cadence. The progression is Ic → V⁷ → VI

g. There is a diminished 7th chord in bar 17, lasting for the entire bar.

EXERCISE 6 (PAGE 15)

The six pieces of music you have just heard are:

Track 6a:

This is minor (note the B naturals – the sharpened 7th).

Track 6b:

This is bitonal. If you rushed to an answer on bars 1 to 4, you might think it is major. However, whereas the LH is firmly in C major, the RH is in A♭ major.

Track 6c:

This is modal. It sounds like A minor, but there are no G#s so it is actually Aeolian, or modal minor.

Track 6d:

This is straightforward C major.

Track 6e:

This is whole-tone music. There is no real sense of a tonal centre, but neither are there any semitones to create a truly atonal dissonance.

Track 6f:

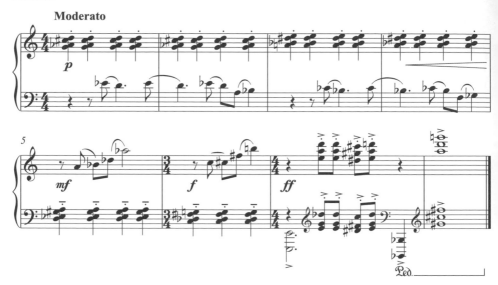

This is atonal. Note the harsh semitones that never resolve.

EXERCISE 7 (PAGE 15)

The four pieces of music that you have just heard are:

Track 7a:

This modulates to the relative minor key of E minor.

Track 7b:

This modulates to the subdominant key of C major.

Track 7c:

This modulates to the dominant key of D major.

Track 7d:

This modulates to the tonic minor key of G minor.

The music for the piece you have just heard is:

Answers

a. Dominant pedal
b. Circle of 5ths harmony
c. Tonic pedal note
d. Suspension.

EXERCISE 9 (PAGES 16–17)

Here are the six different versions of the missing bar 3:

Answers for specimen questions

QUESTION 1 (PAGES 18–19)

a. Brass
b. The bass line falls with a chromatic scale
c. French horns
d. Timpani and cymbals
e. The dominant or 5th
f. Version iii
g. Snare drum (or side drum)
h. The harmony of the main theme is diatonic in the first half and chromatic in the second half
i. Perfect.

a. Organ
b. 3rd
c. A rising minor arpeggio
d. Conquest
e. Melisma
f. The complete pattern is:

g. Minor.

a. A rising minor arpeggio
b. The missing bar is:

c. Harpsichord (piano in some recordings)
d. In bar 17 it is a minor chord, which turns into a major chord in bar 18
e. Oboe and french horn.

a. Timpani
b. Dominant 7th/V⁷ (1 mark for dominant, a second if you spotted the 7th)
c. A diminished 7th
d. Tonic (1 mark) in second inversion (1 mark), or Ic
e. A harmonic (1 mark) minor (1 mark)
f. D minor, or the relative minor
g. An imperfect cadence (or IVb → V)
h. A perfect cadence (1 mark) in B♭ major (1 mark), or the subdominant.

a. Octaves (not monophonic)
b. Minor
c. 'Corals' (the first time the word comes in both verses)
d. First time: upper instrument – oboe; lower instrument – clarinet. Second time: upper instrument – flute; lower instrument – bassoon
e. Rising minor triad and falling octave
f. A solo cello.

a. A circle of 5ths progression (harmonic sequence)

b. The following observations score a mark (maximum of 3):
- Melody played octave lower/in tenor register
- Melody played by the cellos
- Rising scale heard in clarinets (in octaves)
- Sustained chordal accompaniment
- Harmony played by woodwind and horns

c. The following observations score a mark (maximum of 3):
- Melody initially played by violas and bassoon in unison
- Second half of theme played by violins and violas in octaves
- Staccato scales played in semiquavers as accompanying figure
- Accompaniment figure initially played on strings and then flutes
- Bass line played pizzicato by basses (and cellos)

d. The following observations score a mark (maximum of 3):
- Melody played by violins
- New accompaniment figure of conjunct demisemiquavers
- Accompaniment figure used in dialogue between all four woodwinds
- Flute plays a trill at the end of the passage
- Accompanying strings play pizzicato chords.

Glossary

A capella. Unaccompanied vocal music.

Anacrusis. The note or notes that form an upbeat (or upbeats) to the first downbeat of a phrase.

Anticipation. A note played immediately before the chord to which it belongs, so creating a dissonance with the current chord.

Antiphony. A technique where two instrumental groups or two choirs alternate in dialogue.

Appoggiatura. An ornamental note that falls on the beat as a dissonance and then resolves by step onto the main note.

Arco – Bow. As a performance direction in string music, it indicates a change to bowing after the use of another technique, such as **pizzicato**.

Articulation. The manner in which a series of notes are played with regards to their separation or connection – for example, staccato (separated) or legato (connected).

Atonal. Western art music that wholly or largely does not use keys or modes.

Augmentation. The lengthening of rhythmic values of a previously heard melody (e.g. in a fugue), or the widening of an interval.

Augmented 6th chord. A chromatic chord which, in root position, spans the interval of an augmented 6th, e.g. A♭–F♯. The chord also includes the major 3rd above the root (and sometimes also the perfect 5th or augmented 4th, known as German and French augmented 6ths, respectively).

Auxiliary note. A non-harmony note which is a step above (upper auxiliary) or below (lower auxiliary) the harmony note and returns to it.

Binary form. Two-part structure (AB), usually with both sections repeated.

Bitonal/polytonal. Bitonal music uses two different keys simultaneously; polytonal can refer to music using any number of keys greater than one. Clashing keys can be used to symbolise conflict in a drama, for example in Britten's *Billy Budd*.

Cadence. A pair of chords signifying the end of a phrase in tonal music. See also **imperfect cadence, interrupted cadence, perfect cadence** and **plagal cadence**.

Cadenza. A showy passage for a soloist, usually without accompaniment, most commonly found towards the end of the first movement of a concerto.

Canon. A strict form of imitation, often lasting for a substantial passage or entire piece, where the second part is an exact (or almost exact) copy of the first, even if at a different pitch.

Chord extension. Chords which add additional 3rds to the third and fifth degree of a triad, creating a 7th, 9th, 11th or 13th.

Chromatic. The use of non-diatonic notes (notes which are not in the current key). Chromatic notes or chromatic passages are often used for expressive purposes.

Circle of 5ths. A series of chords whose roots are each a 5th lower (or a 4th higher) than the previous one. For example, Em–Am–Dm–G–C.

Coda. A passage (usually relatively short), concluding a piece of music.

Codetta. A passage concluding one section of a piece of music.

Col legno. A string technique of playing with the wood of the bow.

Compound time/metre. Time signature in which the beat divides into three: $\frac{6}{8}, \frac{9}{8}, \frac{12}{8}$.

Con fuoco. Played with a combination of force and speed.

Con sordino. An instruction to the performer to play with a mute.

Conjunct. A conjunct melody moves by step (i.e. in major or minor seconds) rather than by larger intervals. Opposite of **disjunct**.

Consonant. Intervals or chords which are stable and sound pleasant (for example, unisons, 3rds, 6ths), as opposed to its opposite, dissonant.

Continuo. Short for 'basso continuo', the continuo instruments form the accompaniment in Baroque music. It may include instruments such as the harpsichord (capable of playing full harmony) and a cello or bassoon reinforcing the bass line.

Contrary motion. Movement of two parts in opposite directions to each other.

Counter-melody. An independent melody which complements a more prominent theme.

Counterpoint/contrapuntal. The simultaneous combination of two or more melodies that usually have different rhythms.

Cross rhythm. The use of two or more very different rhythms simultaneously in different parts. One rhythm may imply one metre (or time signature), while another implies a different one.

Da capo aria. Common aria form of Baroque opera and sacred music. ABA shape, with Da Capo instruction at the end of the B section. The singer may add ornamentation during the repeat.

Development. The central section of a sonata form movement, which elaborates on the material stated in the **exposition**.

Diatonic. Using notes that belong to the current key.

Diminished 7th. A four-note chord made up of a diminished triad plus a diminished 7th above the root. Diminished 7ths usually function as dominants of the following chord, with the root of the chord omitted in favour of the minor 9th.

Diminution. The shortening of rhythmic values of a previously heard melody.

Disjunct. A disjunct melody moves by intervals larger than a 2nd. Opposite of **conjunct**.

Dissonance. Two or more sounds that give the effect of a clash. Any note not a minor or major 3rd or 6th, perfect 5th, unison or perfect octave above the lowest part sounding is strictly a dissonance.

Divisi. Whereby a single part played by multiple musicians is split into two or more lines.

Dominant. The fifth degree of a major or minor scale.

Dominant 7th. A four-note chord built on the dominant (5th) note of the scale. It includes the dominant triad plus a minor 7th above the root.

Double stopping. A string technique of playing more than one string at a time. Also triple and quadruple stopping.

Enharmonic equivalent. The same pitch notated in two different ways, e.g. B♭ and A♯.

Exposition. The first section of a sonata form movement, which establishes the key and states the musical material to be developed later in the movement.

False relation. A chromatic contradiction between two notes sounded simultaneously and in different parts. For example, a G♮ against a G♯.

Falsetto. This involves the singing of notes above the normal range of the human voice, normally by male singers.

Fugue. A type of piece in which a theme called a **subject** is treated in imitation by all the parts (usually with short passages called 'episodes' from which it is absent, for relief and contrast).

Glissando. A slide between two notes.

Ground bass. Repeating bass, usually four or eight bars in length, with changing music in the other parts. Popular in Baroque music.

Harmonics. A technique of lightly touching a string on a string instrument to produce an artificial high sound (sometimes rather flute-like in quality).

Harmonic rhythm. The rate at which harmony changes in a piece.

Hemiola. The articulation of two units of triple time (*strong-weak-weak*, *strong-weak-weak*) as three units of duple time (*strong-weak*, *strong-weak*, *strong-weak*).

Heterophonic. A texture in which different versions of the same melody are heard simultaneously.

Homophonic. A texture in which one part has a melody and the other parts accompany. In contrast to a polyphonic texture, in which each part has independent melodic interest.

Imitation. A contrapuntal device in which a distinct melodic idea in one part is immediately copied by another part, often at a different pitch, while the first part continues with other music. The imitation is not always strict, but the basic melodic and rhythmic outline should be heard.

Imperfect cadence. An open-ended or inconclusive cadence ending with the dominant chord (V). The preceding chord is usually I, II or IV.

Interrupted cadence. A cadence intended to create surprise or suspense, usually consisting of chord V followed by chord VI.

Leading note. The seventh degree of a major or minor scale.

Leger line. Additional lines used above or beneath the stave to represent notes that fall outside of its range.

Libretto. The script or words for a dramatic work that is set to music (e.g. an opera, musical or **oratorio**).

Mediant. The third degree of a major or minor scale.

Melisma. A technique in vocal music, where a single syllable is set over a number of notes in the melody. Such a passage may be described as 'melismatic'.

Middle-eight. A passage that may be used in popular music forms, describing a section (usually consisting of eight bars and containing different music) that prepares the return of the main section.

Mode. Seven-note scales that can be created using only the white notes of a piano keyboard. The dorian can be played beginning on D (i.e. D–E–F–G–A–B–C–D), the mixolydian on G, the aeolian on A and the ionian on C. These interval patterns can then be transposed to any other note. For example, dorian beginning on G (or G dorian) would be G–A–B♭–C–D–E–F–G.

The modes used in 16th-century church music came to interest later composers looking for an alternative to the major–minor tonal system and have been explored in recent times by various classical, jazz and popular musicians.

Modulation. The process of changing key.

Monophonic. A musical texture that uses a single melodic line.

Mordent. A melodic ornament of two types: a) the lower mordent consists of the written note, the note a step below it and the written note again; b) the upper mordent consists of the written note, the note a step above it and the written note again.

Motif. A short but distinctive musical idea that is developed in various ways in order to create a longer passage of music.

Multi-track recording. A method of recording (normally for popular music) that allows sound sources to be recorded separately and later combined.

Obbligato. Used in Baroque music to denote an instrumental solo part which must be included.

Octave. The interval that encompasses 12 semitones.

Oratorio. A concert piece for choir, soloists and orchestra.

Ostinato. A repeating melodic, harmonic or rhythmic **motif**, heard continuously throughout part or the whole of a piece.

Overdubbing. A recording technique where an additional musical part is recorded to a previously recorded track. This technique is often used by pop musicians to create additional sounds and add more instruments to an existing recording.

Passing note. A non-harmony note approached and quitted by step in the same direction, often filling in a melodic gap of a 3rd (e.g. between G and B, where both G and B are harmony notes).

Pedal note. A sustained or continuously repeated pitch, often in the bass, that is heard against changing harmonies. A pedal on the fifth degree of the scale (known as the dominant pedal) tends to generate excitement, while a pedal on the key note (known as the tonic pedal) tends to create a feeling of repose.

Perfect cadence. Chord V or V7 followed by chord I at the end of a phrase – appropriate where some degree of finality is required.

Periodic phrasing. Balanced phrases of regular lengths (usually two, four or eight bars).

Polyrhythm. The use of more than one rhythm at the same time, often implying the presence of different metres.

Phrasing. In performance the execution of longer groups of notes which follow natural patterns of the music. **Articulation** may be used to refer to phrasing over a shorter group of notes. Phrases may be indicated by the composer but the skill and judgement of the performer is also important in creating a successful performance.

Pizzicato. A direction to pluck, instead of bow, string(s) on a violin, viola, cello or double bass.

Plagal cadence. Chord IV followed by chord I at the end of a phrase.

Polyphonic. A texture consisting of two or more equally important melodic lines heard together. In contrast to a homophonic texture, in which one part has the melody and the other parts accompany. The term polyphonic has a similar meaning to contrapuntal, but is more often used for vocal rather than instrumental music.

Ponticello. See **sul ponticello**.

Portamento. A slide between two notes.

Power chord. A term used in popular music to refer to a chord for guitar that omits the 3rd of the triad. It therefore contains a bare interval of a 5th.

Recapitulation. The final section of a sonata form movement, which restates material from the **exposition** in the tonic key.

Recitative. A technique in opera and oratorio where the singer conveys the text in a speech-like manner. This is normally used to cover narrative effectively and contrasts with arias which are much more lyrical.

Register. A specific part of the range of a voice or instrument.

Relative major and minor. Keys that have the same key signature but a different scale (e.g. F major and D minor, both with a key signature of one flat). A relative minor is three semitones lower than its relative major.

Riff. In popular music styles, a short repeating phrase.

Ritornello. In Baroque music, the repeated tutti section used as a refrain; most often in the first or last movement of a concerto, or in arias or choral works.

Rubato. The alteration of rhythm, particularly in a melodic line, by lengthening and shortening notes but keeping an overall consistent tempo.

Scherzo. A fast piece usually in triple time. Often the third movement in a traditional symphony.

Scotch snap. A two-note dotted rhythm which has the shorter note on the beat. Usually an on-beat semiquaver followed by an off-beat dotted quaver. Also known as lombardic rhythm.

Seconday 7th. Diatonic chords of the 7th other than dominant 7ths.

Segue. The continuation of one section or movement to another without a break. In popular albums, this refers to one track immediately following its predecessor.

Sequence. Immediate repetition of a melodic or harmonic idea at a different pitch, or a succession of different pitches.

Serialism. A system of composing **atonal** music using a predetermined series of the 12 chromatic notes to guarantee equality of all pitches.

Sonata form. The most common structure for the first movement (and often other movements) of sonatas, symphonies, concertos and chamber works in the Classical period and later. The essence of sonata form is the use of two contrasting tonal centres (tonic and either dominant or another closely related key, such as the relative major) in a first section called the **exposition**; the use of a wider range of keys to create tension and excitement in a central section called the **development**; and a **recapitulation** in which music from the exposition is repeated in the tonic key.

Spiccato. Separated string playing, where the instrument is played staccato by bouncing the bow off the string.

Staccatissimo. Very **staccato**.

Staccato. Method of playing a note so that it is shortened and detached.

Strophic. A song in which the music is repeated for each verse; for example, a hymn.

Subdominant. The fourth degree of a major or minor scale.

Subject. One of the sections in the exposition of a movement in **sonata form**.

Submediant. The sixth degree of a major or minor scale.

Sul ponticello. A string technique of playing close to the bridge.

Suspension. A suspension occurs at a change of chord, when one part hangs on to (or repeats) a note from the old chord, creating a dissonance, after which the delayed part resolves by step (usually down) to a note of the new chord.

Syncopation. Placing the accents in parts of the bar that are not normally emphasised, such as on weak beats or between beats, rather than in the expected place on strong beats.

Ternary form. A three-part musical structure in which a middle section is flanked by two identical or very similar passages. The form can be represented by the letters ABA, or ABA1 if there are differences in the A section when it returns.

Tessitura. A specific part of a singer's or instrument's range. For example a 'high tessitura' indicates a high part of the range.

Through-composed. A stage work (opera or musical) in which the music is not split into seperate numbers. Also a song in which there is different music composed for each verse.

Tierce de Picardie. A major 3rd in the final tonic chord of a passage in a minor mode.

Transposition. The process of writing or performing music at a higher or lower pitch than the original.

Tremolo. A rapid and continuous repetition of a single note or two alternating notes.

Trill. An ornament in which two adjacent notes rapidly and repeatedly alternate (the note bearing the trill sign and the one above it).

Tritone. An interval that is equivalent to three tones (an augmented 4th or dimished 5th).

Turn. A four-note ornament that 'turns' around the main note. It starts on the note above, drops to the main note, drops to the note below and then returns to the main note.

Tutti. Italian for 'all' – a term that refers to the full ensemble, or a passage of music intended for full ensemble.

Unison. Simultaneous performance of the same note or melody by two or more players or singers.

Vibrato. Small but fast fluctuations in pitch of a note to add warmth and expression.

Voicing. The arrangement of pitches within a chord to create a particular texture.

Whole-tone scale. A scale in which the interval between every successive note is a whole tone.

Word painting. A technique of setting text in which the sound or movement implied by a word or phrase is imitated by the music (e.g. a falling phrase for 'dying').